Secret Journeys of the Soul

© Copyright 2005 Marjorie Sutton.
All rights reserved. No part of this publication may be reproduced, stored in a retrieval system, or transmitted, in any form or by any means, electronic, mechanical, photocopying, recording, or otherwise, without the written prior permission of the author.

Note for Librarians: a cataloguing record for this book that includes Dewey Decimal Classification and US Library of Congress numbers is available from the Library and Archives of Canada. The complete cataloguing record can be obtained from their online database at:
www.collectionscanada.ca/amicus/index-e.html
ISBN 1-4120-4517-7

TRAFFORD *Offices in Canada, USA, Ireland and UK*

This book was published *on-demand* in cooperation with Trafford Publishing. On-demand publishing is a unique process and service of making a book available for retail sale to the public taking advantage of on-demand manufacturing and Internet marketing. On-demand publishing includes promotions, retail sales, manufacturing, order fulfilment, accounting and collecting royalties on behalf of the author.

Book sales for North America and international:
Trafford Publishing, 6E–2333 Government St.,
Victoria, BC V8T 4P4 CANADA
phone 250 383 6864 (toll-free 1 888 232 4444)
fax 250 383 6804; email to orders@trafford.com

Book sales in Europe:
Trafford Publishing (UK) Ltd., Enterprise House, Wistaston Road Business Centre,
Wistaston Road, Crewe, Cheshire CW2 7RP UNITED KINGDOM
phone 01270 251 396 (local rate 0845 230 9601)
facsimile 01270 254 983; orders.uk@trafford.com
Order online at:
trafford.com/04-2325

10   9   8   7   6   5   4   3   2

Secret Journeys of the Soul

MARJORIE SUTTON

TRAFFORD

Softly I come to thee at dead of night
To see the tears still wet upon thy face
And swiftly I bear thee to a far and secret place
Beyond the stars, where,
In some crystal, perfumed bower,
For one brief, enchanted hour
We speak of hope and a love well spent
Of happiness and a deep content,
Of playing our parts in the Eternal Plan
The mysteries of God and man…….

Until, renewed, I bring you to your earthly home
To dream once more of dreams to come…….
And I, with love, can take my leave
Hoping that you will not grieve
For love will always find a way
Through every step of every day……

Dream on my sweet and precious flower
And we'll await that heavenly hour
When work is done and you and I
Will speak once more……. Love's lullaby

Down To Earth

It all began on the day I was born. For something to begin, something else had to end, for that is the way of things but that ending and that beginning still leaves questions of such awesome proportions that despite even my extraordinary awareness, much is left unanswered.

The awareness I have, is that of Self, of an intelligence operating now within a human frame, within a structure known as the race of man, inhabiting a planet known as Earth. That same Self had operated in some other life form, on some other planet, in some other time.

I recall as if it were yesterday, just how excited I had been. A pure intelligence in transit, needing no form, moving and living for a space of time in a cocoon of soft white light, a sort of soft but solid energy, completely happy as I knew I was nearing the end of my journey. I had no particular thoughts on my future, all directional mental activity being suspended and normal consciousness dimmed as my new life experience drew near, leaving me only with a high anticipation of a bright future as I eagerly awaited my new incarnation.

I was in a state of complete relaxation, the soft white light holding me enigmatically half way between yesterday and tomorrow. A state which was about to change dramatically, as in the final descent I felt myself gently rolling over and over until I was there, somewhere, waiting; my expectations rising as I anticipated the Great Event. Excitement mounted as I awaited the first sight of my new surroundings, anticipated my first feelings at the beginning of this brand new life form. For some little time I experienced a stillness in my protective cocoon, the soft white light surrounding me with its peace, giving me a sense of suspended animation, as I waited for the light to roll back and my new life to begin.

Then I sensed a change. A sense of nothingness, a flatness, a no-movement sensation which went on for far too long and began to concern me more than a little as I lay at the edge of this new dimension. Just as I began to think that I could contain myself no longer, a corner of my white enclosure peeled away and for the first time I could see out. And what I saw horrified me. This was the planet Earth!

There had been some terrible mistake. This was surely the earth plane. My mind just could not grasp the notion that I was on the planet earth. It was impossible. Not here, not ever again. I knew that I had never ever considered returning to this world. Who in their right mind would ever wish to? The earth was a bleak and a dismal place whose peoples were dominated by ignorance and self-destruction. A place way out in the galaxy, far far away from my home and even farther from my mind when I had set out on my present quest. Still operating as an intelligence rather than as a body I was able to see with my extended vision that which surrounded me as the protective shield peeled back, giving way to grim reality. Everything was grey, colourless, mean.

I was in a small room where three people, two men and a woman sat at a table eating a meal. Another woman, bespectacled and wearing a crossover sleeveless pinnie over a dark dress stood at one corner of the table, dishing the food out. There was no sound, just this brief scenario. People, walls, furniture, all dull and drab and depressing. A few seconds later, in another room in that little house, I was drawn into the life form awaiting me, that of a tiny new born baby. But from that moment on I was conscious only of a great and overwhelming desire to leave this plane.

I had arrived in the middle of a war, the violence and noise impaling my sensitivities but then, when hadn't there been a war raging on earth. I was in shock and the wet cold of the planet seemed to hold me in its embrace. I who had flourished in beauty and colour, joy and love, peace and exploration now found myself in this dismal outreach. I still couldn't quite take it all in and I deliberated between wondering if this had been a deliberate act on the part of my mentors as some sort of challenge or, more probably, negligence in the directional mechanisms. There was no way that I could accept that this had been my intended destination. There was a distinct feeling that, in today's parlance, someone back home had pushed the wrong button and in so doing, my whole future had been compromised.

I knew of Earth. Who didn't! Knew that I had lived on earth before as many of us had for one reason or another but I knew just as surely that I had not intended another incarnation here. This was a young planet whose peoples had not travelled far in their evolution; whose leaders much preferred to govern the masses through ignorance and superstition despite help that had been repeatedly sent to them through highly evolved Others returning to earth to show them the way. A world whose people were hell bent on conflict; seemingly trapped in an endless cycle of mental and physical suicide, dying before they could graduate to the spiritual arena which all beings had to attain in order to achieve spiritual evolution. They seemed doomed to concentrating their efforts in self-perpetuating myths, unable to raise their sights and their ambitions beyond the third dimension. Spiritual to me did not mean godly or holy, simply that which transcended basic physical consciousness.

I then began to wonder again if I was simply kidding myself and that everyone felt like this when taking on another incarnation on earth. There was a terrible sense of confusion whilst my mind raced along fielding a variety of possibilities. It was possible of course that I was no different to anyone else but the knowledge that I had travelled from another place out in space overwhelmed me and I still believed without a doubt that I had been bound for another place in another time.

As always my immediate thought was to the Father, my constant mental companion and confidante in any and every crisis. The Father was not necessarily a man but was a male influence, as far as I am aware without form as we know it; who directed my spiritual path, connecting with me on all levels at all times. There was no religious connotation here but He was the Being on whom I relied totally.

There are no suitable words that could convey my meaning in this three-dimensional world, for the Father is way beyond this and many other dimensions. I was and am locked into that Being for all my foreseeable time. Although as a being I am way below Him in terms of evolution I am nevertheless a fundamental, integral part of Him. My urgent wish was to have Him extricate me from this mess before it was too late for in some inexplicable way I knew there was a time limit if I was to be able to return to my home. Quickly I began sending out vibrational signals into space in the hope that I would be heard, recalled, that a blessed darkness would descend heralding my return journey but to no avail and I began to fear that it was already too late. I was not going to be taken back. I was in this alien place and here I must stay.

As I lay there in total disbelief, I pondered on how this mistake could have happened. Who had been meant to come here and had they arrived at what I had considered to be my appointed destination. And what had been their destiny and would I now have to fulfil it? My mind went round and around over these matters, sometimes hopefully, believing that everything could still be put right but deep within, I had the sinking feeling that now I was here, I was here for as long as it took.

The Father was silent and the silence was ominous. He would never interfere, never intervene for that was not the way of things. Resolve not intervention was the way of all karma but I had hoped for some explanation and the fact that He was silent seemed to me a very powerful message. I was on my own. There would be no turning back and it would be a long time now before I knew just what had happened. As the days went by I was quite convinced that had I been intended for this plane, I would have met by now a member of my own group soul who was also part of the Plan. One who would greet me. One whom I would instantly recognise in their spiritual aspect to confirm, reassure, and make that connection which would set all the other wheels in motion but no one of that nature appeared. Day after day I scrutinised every newcomer and day after day I became more despondent. There had to be a Plan and Players and a Script and instead there was a very real sense for me of being an outsider, a mere spectator of other people's plays which held no interest for me. A visitor from any other world could do as much and then return with the knowledge but I was not a mere visitor.

Taking on another incarnation meant that different Laws were in play, Laws which could not now be altered. Laws that I would have to abide by. I worked it out that my mother had become pregnant and an incarnating soul had chosen her as host, not I, but in the mix up I had to take on that role and the other soul had taken on mine presumably. I was not evolved enough to pretend to know everything but balance has always to be maintained both in the micro and the macro worlds. Mistakes can happen everywhere, nothing is foolproof, that is part of our evolving universe. It was of little comfort for me to acknowledge that in the aeons of eternity which lay before me all things would be put right. Here and now I had to concede that eventually I had to get on with being here.

What the future might hold for me on this strange hostile planet I neither knew nor cared, my mind always occupied as to how I could leave it. Locked into my own sense of oblivion, I did not contemplate the life that might await me; did not see the future outside of the immediate. I was not to know then that my life could and would consist of fantastic, amazing adventures, not just in and concerning this world but in others too. There would be journeys into other dimensions, experiencing other bodies, giving rise to much speculation, contemplation and not a little confusion.

All this was yet to come, my immediate dilemma concentrated my mind on much more pressing problems. Being on your own in an alien place turns you into the alien and the effort of living with this knowledge was to take every ounce of my strength in those early days.

Early Days

My arrival naturally evoked much interest within what turned out to be a large, close-knit family. For those around me, my birth was yet another problem in a war torn world. Another mouth to feed, days and nights to be up, caring for this new little body and wondering perhaps, if it would survive the poverty, the disease, the war. They were not to know the spirit which had come amongst them; the intelligence that could look out of tiny eyes and read their very hearts. They saw only a tiny form, a baby totally dependent on them in every possible physical way and thus, in their eyes a limited intelligence too.

During this time I had no interest in who my parents were or where they were for that matter. I was to discover later that my mother had almost died in giving birth to me and had stayed unconscious for three weeks. My father was a regular soldier, away at the front.

Day after day I watched and waited, hungry for a sign of recognition from one of those who would come into my orbit but matters only became worse. During those dreadful days, when men and women lived their lives against a backdrop of daily suspense and the promise of sudden death, especially for those at the front, I would listen to people. People talking, crying, confiding, confessing. I grew weary and would switch off to everything going on around me. There was no one I could recognise, no one I could turn to. As time went by I would lay for hours watching, observing the people around me, seeing them only as barbarians, closing my eyes in contempt at their mean little claustrophobic lives. Their dreariness threatened to swamp me, each day a joyless repetition of the chores of the day before, accepting what was because they were ignorant of what could be. Nothing changed and the awful thing was, that as things stood, it wasn't destined to.

There was no bonding with this mother I had not seen and there never would be. The woman who cared for me was this other, much older woman, always busy working whilst others came and went; the sometimes bespectacled lady who always wore what I suspected was a floral overall but the colours came across as faded grey and brown. It would be a further two years before I saw colour as colour, so great was the difference between the colours here and the colours I had known.

My grandmother, for that was who the lady in the floral pinnie was, attracted a great many people to her, usually those in need in some way, who every day visited her home. One by one they would peer into my pram and stare at me, shoving their faces into mine making strange gestures with their mouths and even stranger noises. I was not amused. They actually thought that because my physical form was small that I the Self within was small, young, unknowing. I wanted to scream and shout at them. "Look at Me. Really look at Me." But even if I could have spoken, what would be the point. When you cannot see, you cannot see.

As I lay locked into this little life form sometimes in it's pram, sometimes lying swathed in a shawl on an easy chair I would watching the comings and goings of daily life. No one tried to communicate with the essential me. No one knew that it was possible even. Although I am now ashamed to admit to it, I held them all in complete and utter contempt. As yet I was still a small baby very much operating in my astral body and withdrawing into that body meant that I slept a great deal. Withdrawing into my astral awareness enabled me to venture to another spot, rather more ethereal, away from the streets of terraced houses that I never seemed to leave. Living in this other world was automatic for me and I was quite safe. I would be in a state of separateness, surrounded by colour, away from all fear.

When I decided to remain physically conscious but use my astral facilities I was able to use my astral sight in quite a different way. I was able to see others and myself, physically and astrally. Whereas the physical body has two receptors for sight, the eyes, the astral body has receptors throughout, so one can see in all directions at once. I could also will myself 'out' and look 'into' myself. On one occasion I looked within myself to see what they would see if they could use their own astral faculty to see me. What I saw was not what I had expected. It gave me quite a jolt.

As I looked deep into my own physical eyes, I saw a very old woman, whose face despite her age was quite unlined. A strict authoritarian personality looked back. I saw her head and shoulders as in a portrait. She was dressed in black with a large white collar, a tight fitting white headdress that completely covered her head, coming to a point at the front. She was 94 years of age and I suspected a Belgian influence. Now who on earth was this I wondered. She had appeared in my vision as one of two possibilities. Either she had been a past incarnation, perhaps someone from the Low Countries by birth, or she was me as I would be when this incarnation was over. That thought, of staying here that long, gave me no comfort at all and I returned rapidly to seeing in my limited physical being. I did not wish to even think of staying here for such a period of time.

The weeks and the months passed by and I felt weary of the comings and goings of people. My grandmother was akin to the community nurse, always on call, the kettle always on the boil, no one ever turned away. She was the confidante of the whole neighbourhood, combining the roles of assistant midwife, counsellor and first aider when people couldn't always afford to go to the doctor with minor ailments. During these times I could be relied upon not to interrupt, winge or distract the adults in any way. People would comment on what a good baby I was. Little did they know that I was hardly ever there! My own astral world was preferable to anything here.

There were many who would come to her after receiving bad news from the front and she was always ready to listen and give support, saying little but always it seemed that which was needed. In between times she worked constantly at her household chores, fiercely houseproud.

I recall one day when a young woman came into the room and began to tell her tale of woe, her tears falling as grandmother gave her a cup of tea and settled her down. Her story was not unique. Her husband was at the front and she had been seen out with another man. She had been accused by her in-laws of betraying her husband's trust, of adultery and now she was an outcast in her own family. I listened incredulous as the tale unfolded and more tea was poured, my grandmother giving her the benefit of the doubt, drying her tears, holding the woman close, dispensing her own particular form of wisdom.

The woman was lying and she was lying most of all to herself. She was determined to believe her version of events, as she could not accept herself what she had done. Sadly she was missing the opportunity to make a clean breast of it to someone not immediately involved with her family and who might have been able to get her back on track. She went away smiling and never came back again. It was all so dreary. Why didn't these people ever learn? More karma and future upset which could have been dealt with, had been put on hold to grow and fester within her heart and mind and no doubt she would continue lying to herself and believing her lies no matter what. This woman had been determined to fool the deeper self but that couldn't be. One day the deeper self would offer it up again to be resolved and who knew how much damage it would cause in the meantime. And would the woman recognise how much damage the past could inflict on the future, even the distant future. I feared not.

I would look at my grandmother who refused to judge anyone. She was nobody's fool and knew more than most that the whole truth was seldom a guest at the wedding and probably recognised the lie just as I had. But as always she had not been found wanting in her compassion, her willingness to help and she had done all that was humanly possible. The terribleness of war made people behave out of character sometimes; could make fools of us all. My poor grandmother. Two world wars, seven children, an eighth who had died after a few months and now me who, unlike her, continued to judge my fellow beings and switch off when they annoyed me with their foolishness. Me who was only marking time until I could return home.

But time was marching on. On the physical side I was quick to adjust, walking and talking at ten months and as time went on people thought me such a clever child. Clever but quiet. I would sit for hours with a book on my lap but once again I wasn't there. I would withdraw to far away places. Grandmother for her part was always happy for me to be at rest, behaving myself, no trouble in a world that promised trouble every time the postman knocked and shuffled his way down the narrow lobbies of the little houses. The kettle was always singing on the hob in her little house at eleven o'clock every morning just in case there was bad news for someone in the street.

The biggest problem was that there was no one for me to communicate with, not physically but telepathically. No one understood me. More to the point, they all ignored me as an intelligent being that is, and life was extremely lonely and frustrating. I was about fifteen months old when I first began to get sick. Not surprisingly my inner conflict now began to manifest in my physical body. Not surprisingly it was concentrated in my chest, the heart center. Pleurisy, pneumonia, double pneumonia, bronchitis. I remember it was extremely painful and I would become extremely hot. There being no antibiotics in those days for this condition I would have to stay in bed day after day until the crisis passed and all the time my grandmother would be with me, day and night.

I can recall clearly when I was two and again going through a crisis. People were around the bed and in the gloom of a single nightlight I could see my grandparents comforting each other. Some of those present were crying and one of them said to my grandfather, "I don't think she'll make it this time Joe. She's going to die." And she burst out sobbing. The rest followed her example. I did not understand what was meant by dying but it was obviously not to be recommended and I was not too impressed. As always I turned to the Father. "Oh Father, please, please take me home. I don't want to die. It sounds terrible. Please, please take me home." I was terrified. A couple of days later and I awoke again. I was still here. At least I hadn't died even if He hadn't taken me home, He had done half the things I had asked. Life would continue. I sighed and went back to sleep.

My mother and I never bonded. All her thoughts were for my father who had been parachuted into Arnhem which was understandable to a point. Perhaps the difficult birth had played a part in her rejection of me or perhaps she just wished that I had never happened. Whatever the reason behind it all, a solemn faced, blue-eyed child with platinum curly hair falling about her shoulders couldn't reach her, then or ever after.

My grandparents were the ones I had to turn to for help and love and food but my depressions returned and with them my illnesses. As I grew older, into my third and fourth years I would be taken for a special trip into the town but I was always 'fainting' and they would end up having to get a bus and bring me back. Although I was gradually being absorbed more and more into my physical body I could still leave at will or when I became tired of the adult world around me. Of course they did not know this and the good doctor only knew what they told him of my physical symptoms as they perceived them, so now the doctor feared that I had a heart problem too and ordered bed rest. Poor man. He did his best but there was nothing they could find physically that could be treated any other way. My grandmother was informed that she would never rear me. I was a fragile child and needed much attention. I didn't understand all that. What I did was natural and I couldn't understand what all the fuss was about. I also knew that I could not explain to anyone because of their limited understanding. I truly believed that they would have put me away as some bad person or they would become very fearful of me as a strange being in their midst. As always with ignorance at the helm, the seas of superstition were the only ones travelled.

It was about this time that I began to fall down stairs with monotonous regularity. At first I thought I must have tripped and then I realised that I was having a problem with my loose etheric body. After this had occurred a couple of times I carefully observed what was happening. I noticed that as I approached a particular stair, for some reason my foot was going through the stair, etherically that is, on each occasion, causing me to stumble. I could both see and feel what was happening.

The etheric is the double of the physical so it looked just like my physical foot and it felt as if my foot was penetrating cool water as the etheric foot went through the stairtread. At the same time I could see my physical foot resting on the stairtread. This double take meant that I did not concentrate fully on manouvering the steep stairs and so in the resulting faltering hesitation, I would stumble and fall. Having done this a few times I tried to walk down two stairs at once, thus avoiding the difficult one but my legs were too little and I fell anyway.

It took me some time to work out why this particular stair was causing me problems and then I realised the power of the mind had a big part to play even in this dimension. After the first time I fell, I was waiting for it to happen again, imagining it happening again and of course it did. I was creating my own reality. After that I made sure that my thoughts as I began my descent of the stairs were of complete oneness in my energy fields and the tumbling stopped.

My grandmother however had an idea that I was somewhat of a fey child. She knew that I could read although I had never been taught. She also knew that I could 'see' but not just what. She believed very much in a life after death and of the power of loved ones who had passed on, being able to communicate. She had seen in that way herself but her deep devotion to the catholic faith ensured that she never spoke about such things unless in 'safe' company, just in case anyone got the wrong idea.

In the days when television was unheard of and the war was still being reckoned, many tales were told around the fire in the evening, of strange dreams and events that had saved someone's life or predicted a death. Grandfather would speak knowingly of the Angel of Mons and grandmother would speak quietly of the people who she and her sisters had seen before each death in the family, when they were small.

Once, her late father had returned to warn her of her mother's impending early death. Another time it had been a nun dressed in the habit of the home of the Little Sisters of Mercy who appeared on the stairs as she and her sisters went to bed. Later on that night, a knock had come at the front door and there had stood a nun to inform them of the death of a relative in their Home. Everyone listened intently, each having their own interpretation and questions, remembering others who had had similar experiences. There was always a house full as in any large family and I was able to stay up, usually in hiding under the table or behind a large armchair doing my usual impression of a mouse, which meant that they usually forgot I was there.

After one of these evening sessions my grandmother accompanied me to my bedroom where she bade me listen carefully. I stared at her solemnly whilst she spoke. She was most concerned about my future in some way. She went on to tell me that I would 'see' one day and that when I did I should not be afraid. 'The dead never came back to harm anyone. I should just listen to them and take heed.' She left me then and went downstairs. I nearly died! The thought of someone dead appearing to me was almost more than I could bear. I got undressed and jumped into bed pulling the covers over my head, sweating with fear. I still hadn't understood that the dead they spoke of were those I knew as just ordinary people now living in another dimension busy getting on with their real lives. I didn't really know what they meant by 'the dead' and like anyone ignorant of the true concept behind any situation, I panicked as my imagination took over. It was a long time before sleep claimed me that night.

My family were also friendly with a man and his son who were Spiritualists, beautiful people, loving and gentle, who showed my family how to communicate with spirit by 'rocking' the table. On occasions, everyone would sit round and place their fingertips on the heavy oak table and concentrate on making contact with those 'beyond the veil'. Someone would ask a question and the table would rock once for yes, two for no. Now this was a stout oak table and it really did move. I would stand there, my head just reaching above the table and watch with interest, no real understanding of what they were doing. I recognised what they were trying to do of course but I didn't understand why they went to all that trouble.

Invariably when questions were asked and the answers did not immediately describe the 'entity' communicating, I would pipe up and tell them who it was, although of course these people had returned long before my arrival and I had never met them. All I had to do was tune in telepathically and pass on their information. In this way I learned that the people of earth were moving on a little but as always I expected too much of them. I assumed that they now did believe that contact was possible with those in other dimensions but they didn't really, it was more wishful thinking than anything else. I believed in my childlike way that they would realise more about me after these sessions too but they seemed to ignore the fact that I always 'knew' who was there. Instead they would dismiss it as strange, their eyes narrowing as they studied me before shrugging it off.

But beyond all this my grandmother knew. She wasn't sure what she knew and how much I knew but that I did know hadn't escaped her. Everything she did for me she did with true love. I was very special to my grandparents and she in particular formed my future values. This was the lady who had been with me from the outset and whom I had rejected so determinedly as yet another 'barbaric' person. Someone I had not recognised, yet was now growing to rely on entirely. I loved her very dearly and I grew never to question the wisdom of her words. From now on she would be my shining star, whose tinsel would never tarnish, whose flame would never diminish, whose memory would never fade.

My father had returned from the war, leaving the army he had chosen 16 years earlier. I believe this was because my mother would not move away from her roots and that decision was in time, to create a perpetual atmosphere of bitterness and recrimination within their home. I remained living with my grandparents, most people even calling me by their surname. At first, when I knew that my father was returning and that my mother had sorted a house out, I had looked forward with great excitement to joining them. My grandmother had taken me to see the house and I had sat there proudly in a new fireside chair, looking at all the shiny new furniture, thinking that this was to be my new home too. As always it was my grandmother who had to let me down gently. I caught the smirk on my mother's face as my grandmother explained that I had to stay with her and grandfather for the time being. A knife seemed to be twisting in my tummy. My mother was congratulating herself on getting her own way. She would have my father to herself. I was not a part of her future plans. She actually enjoyed seeing my bitter disappointment and confusion. She was jealous of me.

As the taxi took us back home, for I was recovering yet again from another bout of pneumonia, I realised with a great sadness, that my mother didn't want me. Although very young, I could of course see into her heart and the shock was truly great. As indeed was the hurt. How could they not want me? A product of their love surely. I knew that I was what was classed as a pretty little girl and yet they didn't want me. What would have happened had I been handicapped? I felt cold for a long time after that.

When I was five years old I became so depressed that I could not eat, I had been very ill yet again but this time my recovery seemed never to be. I could see the worry on my grandparent's faces but despite my love for them I so desperately wanted to go home. A bed was always brought downstairs for me when I was ill, ensuring that I was kept in the same temperature day and night. It also meant that I was never alone for a minute, so deep was their concern.

Early one morning as my grandmother prepared breakfast in the kitchen, my grandfather came downstairs and as always, asked her how the night had gone. My grandmother just shook her head, tears on her face. I looked away not wishing to see her distress acknowledging to myself that I was being thoroughly selfish in my own desires but the emotional pain I was going through seemed just too much to bear. My loneliness had reached breaking point. The only thing which concerned me, was my existence in this realm. I was here all alone and for what reason? Everything was still beyond my understanding.

My grandfather went through into the yard and I assumed he was going to the outside toilet. Lost in my own thoughts I did not hear him return until he called my name yet again. "Madge, Madge…What do you think?" What did I think about what? I sighed deeply and turned and took the proffered plate of toast from his hand. But soon I pushed the plate away. Food was not what I wanted or needed. I heard my grandmother's hushed voice from the kitchen. "What's happening Joe?"

"She's not bothering lass," He sounded so low. I looked at him again. "I'm not hungry." I turned my head to the wall. "But what do you think Madge?" I just looked at him whilst my grandmother hovered at a distance.

"She can't see it Joe, she's lying down and she can't see it." Grandmother was twisting the tea towel in her hand now leaning against the doorjamb. Grandad looked at me. "Can you not see it Madge? Here, lean up and see what I've brought you." Grandad's face was a mixture of eagerness to get my reaction and a desperate longing for everything to be all right. Wearily I leant on my elbow, propping myself up, staring up into his face. "No Madge. Down here, on the floor." His finger pointed downwards. I could see my grandmother, clutching the kitchen towel to her chest, now, holding her breath. I looked and could not believe my eyes. There, sitting on the floor was the tiniest most beautiful cocker spaniel puppy, no bigger than the size of his hand. "He's yours Madge. What do you think?"

Delight flooded my heart, my eyes I knew shone with love and excitement. Here was another with whom I could communicate and the bond between us was immediate. "Lift it up onto the bed Joe then she can feel it," whispered my grandmother and my grandfather placed it gently as any woman, on my lap. I can still recall the exquisite pleasure I felt that morning. It was pure joy. I reached out for my plate of toast. I now had something to live for. Later as I watched my grandfather preparing for work my love for him just flowed.

Marjorie Sutton

Here was a man's man and no mistake. A man who had won the George Cross in the first world war for bravery beyond the call of duty, still smoking Captain Full Strength despite being gassed in the war and whose career in the army he loved so much had been stopped so completely, still capable of loving and caring. I watched as he wrapped his muffler about his neck and put on his bicycle clips. His job as a storekeeper down at the docks was a lowly one for such a proud man but he was not so proud that he didn't realise that his money was essential no matter how little. No one could ever take his medals from him and the George Cross! Well, he could always hold his head up high and my grandmother never stopped worshipping him.

He had won the George Cross when, despite coming under heavy fire, he had not left his post. His post being that of being in command of the ammunition wagon pulled by horses. He had stuck it out and desperately needed supplies for the soldiers had got through. He wouldn't have left his beloved horses either to fend for themselves. Such was the measure of the man. No wonder my grandmother adored him.

From that day on, my obsession with leaving this vale of tears receded and Queenie, my little soul mate, as my grandfather named her, after consultation with me of course, was the focus of my life. Grandfather had trained horses and dogs in his time in the army and farm collies outside of it and the animals obviously adored him. Soon Queenie was able to perform so many tricks, she was almost human. That of course was my tongue in cheek thought which I kept firmly to myself. But she and I would sit together by the hearth on many a winter's day, perfectly happy in just being.

When my grandfather went anywhere, we would both follow. He took great pride in teaching me how to look after his animals and birds. He bred chinchillas and had an aviary of brightly coloured budgies and canaries in the yard. By this time I could see colour and the war had ended. The brightly whitewashed yard containing the aviary of brilliant greens and yellows was a good place to be. I thought that I was completely secure in my physical body and whilst I still had no answers as to the why's and the wherefore's of my existence here, I had finally accepted that which couldn't be changed.

There came a day a couple of years later when my wishes to return to my true home were nearly fulfilled. The day had dawned cold and damp and I had been allowed to stay in bed due to a bout of tonsillitis until members of the family had all gone off to work, when I was taken downstairs by my grandmother to have a bath in order to 'freshen me up and make me feel better.' She had locked the front door to stop anyone walking in on us and flames from the fire were dancing up the chimney in front of the tin bath awaiting me. Taking off my nightclothes she proceeded to wash me with a sponge and lots of soapy water. I hadn't actually stepped into the bath because that would be to sit in dirty water she reckoned. Better for me to have a good wash 'through' in the living room than in the cold back kitchen. I remember feeling extremely tired and flopping back against an armchair close by the hearth.

I knew no more until I awoke slowly, aware only of icy cold air on my naked body. Forcing my eyes open with great difficulty I could see my grandmother across from me trying to get up from the chair she had collapsed on and my grandfather swearing loudly as he rushed around opening doors throughout the house. In his fright he was calling her severely for her stupidity. Apparently the fumes from the built up coke fire had built up in the room and enveloped us. If he hadn't returned to collect the lunchbox he had forgotten, probably the only time ever he had left his lunch at home, we would certainly have died.

As I regained full consciousness, my grandmother with tears pouring down her face, dressed me. When I realised what had almost happened I didn't know whether to laugh or cry but prudently did neither. My grandfather was shaking at the realisation of how close we had come to real tragedy as he took the coke off the fire with a shovel and threw it into the yard. Then he took his wife into his arms and hugged her tight, reaching out for me and together we held on tightly to each other. For the first time I accepted unequivocally that I was here to stay.

Settling In

As the years rolled on by, I became more absorbed into the physical and led the life of a normal child, still pretty fragile but never really at death's door again much to the delight of my grandparents. My ailments of childhood, the pain and the torment, dropped away. I no longer scanned those around me and although I knew that I was terribly different in my perceptions of the world, I was as most children are, brainwashed by those around me. The church school that I attended was most assiduous in this direction. I learned about a God I had never heard of and what I learned I did not like but accepted completely that which my elders and, I was assured, most definitely betters, drummed into me.

They did not however manage to remove the Father from my every waking thought and it was to Him I turned for help to get me through most every day. I could not be but afraid of this other God who was petty and picky and who saw my every deed and thought and who would punish me for my childish misconceptions. I seemed to spend my whole life trying to get it right and as one so often does when one tries too hard, getting it hopelessly wrong.

I still hadn't learned that others could not read my thoughts, could not therefore know my intentions as they went about in this solid, dense world. I on the other hand, knowing theirs, would be streets ahead in a conversation, albeit in telepathy and this could lead to much confusion. There was a time when I resorted back to telepathy, resulting in my hardly ever speaking, just looking at people when they spoke to me. For me this was quite normal and a much quicker way of communicating but it caused much alarm in my home for a little time. They thought that I had lost the power of speech and were concerned that my earlier illnesses had left their toll on my brain. Then life rolled on again and I remembered to speak when I was spoken to but my mind to this day leaps ahead too often, chattering away whilst my tongue is stilled. Thoughts are so much more expressive than words and so often there is not a suitable word for that which I would convey.

By this time I was being taken to my parents home for small periods. I now had a younger sister, six years my junior who spent all her time with our parents. My mother had given birth to her at my grandparent's house. I recall being awakened at 7 o'clock one morning with the exciting news that the baby had arrived.

During her pregnancy, my mother had plagued me with dire threats of being thrown under a bus when the new baby arrived. I presume she was under duress at the time. Not unnaturally, at that time I believed her and I began to fret as the time for the birth drew near. I could no longer face food and my little mind was filled with horror every time a bus went down the street. My grandmother, ever alert to the feelings of others brought my mother's attention to my condition. I recall my mother taking me into the parlour and questioning me as to why I would not eat. I explained to her that it was due to my impending demise, whereupon she smirked and said, "Don't be so silly." After some thought she made me promise not to tell anyone what I had told her and in return she promised me that she wouldn't go ahead with her dreadful plans.

She then took me back into the living room and told everyone that I had just been silly and that she had sorted the matter out. Much relieved that I was not going to be thrown under a bus, I recovered my appetite and awaited the coming of the baby with much excitement. My mother had suggested that the baby would be the doll I never had and I had asked her for a black one, so on that morning I ran eagerly to a fireside chair and waited. The midwife duly arrived from the next room where my mother had given birth and placed the tiny bundle in my arms. Pulling back the shawl I gazed on the tiny form. "Oh" I wailed, "It's white." I looked up at the bewildered midwife. "Take it back," I cried. "I don't want a white one. My mummy said it was going to be black." The midwife's face was a picture. My family of course, put me in the doghouse for a week.

Despite my lack of schooling due to illness when very young, I managed to pass my eleven-plus and attended a convent run by nuns. The education was good but I was not terribly interested in most subjects. For a time I appeared to be normal again. It was here I discovered that nuns could and did lie which was an enormous shock and was the beginning of the end for me with the catholic religion. Then puberty arrived and once again I found myself quite often more at home in my astral body. So much so that sometimes when walking to school with my friends I would walk out of the physical as I was busy chatting away and I would hold my breath in despair until the physical caught up. I always felt that it was wrong to do this but it just happened and I would look aghast at my friends, waiting for their condemnation and disapproval but they never mentioned it and just carried on as if nothing had happened.

I didn't realise of course that they had not been aware of what had happened. Everything unnatural was so very natural to me. Even though I knew that those around me were not aware of spiritual matters to the same extent, it never really went into my consciousness, as it should have done. I would think about it as I did my homework. Why didn't they see me stepping out of my body? After all it is quite a big thing and quite unusual and they are spirit too. How could they not see? I would spell it out to myself…Everybody… is…

spirit... occupying... a... physical... body. No matter how low the consciousness, that was a basic premise and that at least they should know intuitively if not consciously. Whether it was my hormones that brought about this confusion with me or whether I became so lonely in my own knowledge, I cannot tell but I would spend hours agonising over the differences between me and them.

Another problem for me at this time was that of becoming very aware of people from other dimensions around me. I could feel them sitting next to me, hear their breathing and generally understood that I was never alone. This I didn't like. Seeing that I had to stay here and continue with my life on this plane, I couldn't see the point of forever being reminded that there were better places to be and a better life to be had elsewhere. It wasn't so much that they were visiting me as much as I had inadvertently opened the door so to speak into their world.

I tried telling my mother about these experiences but she told me not to be silly, as usual. In her opinion, there were things one spoke about and things one didn't. Other worlds, a bit like sex, were taboo, didn't exist and were figments of my imagination. This only served to make me feel even more isolated as I pulled the covers up tight about me in bed as these 'visitors' paid their nightly respects. Having had seven years without incident, spiritually speaking, makes one forgetful of other worlds as this one takes over, so feeling someone sitting on your bed was not conducive to a good night's sleep.

Marjorie Sutton

After all I couldn't see them and this made me afraid as I remembered the usual ghost stories people had told. I used to pray like mad for help but the pressure on the bed would get worse. It was some time later that I realised the extra pressure was help at hand, a reassurance, if you like, that there wasn't a problem but at the time it was scary.

I never did discuss anything with my father. I disliked him as much as he appeared to dislike me and his life in general. Leaving the army had been the worst decision of his life, one from which he never truly recovered. He too had won medals for gallantry and trophies for shooting and life in a small town must have been dreadful after all the military action he had craved and participated in around the world. After brief periods of living with my parents I would return to my grandparent's home with scarcely contained delight. He was the only person I have ever hated. Despite my mother's coldness, he vented his frustration on both of us. Forbidding us to move, speak, listen to the radio or watch the TV for hours until he finally went to the pub. He called my mother bad names and I used to pray that he would leave her. He was so contemptuous and the energies in that little house were horrid when ever he was around.

But life goes on and as a teenager, back with my grandparents, I began again to scan people. I would do it automatically, spontaneously and then I decided to practise more and more. I did this when I was on buses, waiting for buses, walking down the road. I used it as a relief from boredom until it suddenly occurred to me that knowing more than I might otherwise do about people gave me an unfair advantage and somehow it was like an invasion of their privacy. When I realised that whilst my experiments were completely innocent, the whole idea of scanning could be seen as something unpleasant, I stopped. It had also become extremely boring, as most people's lives were pretty much the same.

The same themes were repeated. Lies, deceit, cheating, broken love affairs, suspicion, worry. But then I lived amongst people who were poor, many of whom had had little in the way of education, opportunity or luxury and whose minds never ran across the perimeters of their tiny worlds.

I was back now living with my grandparent's full time and these themes were not repeated in our large family. Little lies perhaps but deceit and cheating, no. My grandmother had always insisted that money was not the root of all evil. Lies were. 'You have to lie to do all the other bad things successfully.' she would say and she insisted we all lived by this dictate.

I believed people to have very small lives, little or no expectations, which I found very sad and so I gave up my addiction to scanning. There was never anything new, never anything earth shattering or amazingly uplifting. Individuals showed tremendous courage in adversity and I had nothing but admiration for those in the human race who keep on keeping on, but on the whole, life on this planet was remaining true to past form. About this time too, I began to become more aware of the needs of my physical body, of the role it had to play and how we had to co-exist or one of us would be very unhappy. I didn't work with my body at this time in the way I realised I had to do later, but I did take great physical care of it. On the basis Lives I have many - Bodies I have one I took a great interest in ensuring as far as I could that after a very dodgy start in this life, my body needed to be strong for the future. I didn't know why but I just went with the urge to become very fit. I had already played tennis and hockey at school and now that I was working I would walk for miles every Sunday with a local walkers club, spending every weekend in the beautiful Lake District. I also joined a gym.

Then I stumbled on a book about Yoga and Yogic breathing. This fascinated me as I had a particular condition which from time to time gave me a great deal of pain and nausea and for which medicine did not have an answer. I began to practise faithfully the excercises in the book for deep relaxation, rushing home from work to spend an hour or so in the privacy of my bedroom learning the art of this deep relaxation. The next time this annoying condition occurred again I put myself to the test. Day after day I tried to put into practise what I had learned so far. It was wonderful. Even though the pain was severe, my earlier concentrated practise was paying off. I was able to relax my body until one day I knew that I had come out of sync. with my physical body and was floating, sort of half in and half out but not totally out.

As this took place, I became aware of the change in what I was feeling in the physical body. The sensation of pain changed to that of colour, a dark grey colour in the region where the pain originated. As I continued, the colour changed to sound that in turn changed in timbre to a dull note that in turn faded away as I withdrew further from the physical. In this conscious state I was completely relaxed and happy. I had no intention of coming out of my body completely but would have allowed this to happen had it happened naturally.

The condition was to return again and again but each episode was better than the last until I lost the condition completely and I realised that I had been healed by this method of deep relaxation. The depth of relaxation had allowed my bodies or energy fields to separate and realign and so I had inadvertently triggered off the healing mechanism within me. When I went nursing a couple of years later I learned that my condition had been muscle spasm and hormonal imbalance which had been corrected simply by relaxing the body in a deep and conscious way, always in control whilst nevertheless going with the flow. I was to remember this many years later when more serious conditions manifested and my understanding of self-healing was made clear to me.

At this time in my life I turned my attention towards a career. There was very little to choose from in my mind. Helping the sick, working with orphaned children. It was my ambition to run a children's home. To this end I would enter the nursing profession. Although I was to marry, un-

Marjorie Sutton

like most women I never gave marriage more than a passing thought. Life for me was about work, about helping others, about making things happen for others, especially children who were handicapped or rejected. Surprisingly, I did not relate at that time to any parallel within myself. I just never considered any other future. For a few years I lived with these aims in sight but events were to overtake me time and time again. Life seemed to get in the way and I like everyone else had to bow to the inevitable. Life on Earth. Good times, bad times. But I seemed to have to concentrate solely on my everyday lifestyle. Altering as it often did from year to year, the spiritual and the mystical gave way to the normal day to day existence the majority of us have to deal with. Marriage, divorce, children, work. I tended to believe that whatever had to be done would be and that I like everyone else would just have to get through it all as best I could. I had no intimation on a particular day in spring that once again changes would take place in my life and the spiritual and the mystical would once more beckon.

The Messenger

On a day in spring news came of the work I was to do in the future. As always with me it came in it's own inimical way. I had just finished a burst of spring cleaning on a particularly lovely morning and was looking forward to a long lazy bath before venturing out in the afternoon. I was having a day off from my work as a nurse at the local hospital and pleased that the day was so warm and that spring had finally arrived.

I hadn't been in the bath two minutes when a voice spoke close in my ear. 'Go to the church.' You must be joking I protested. I'm going to relax for a long time, and I snuggled down in the water. But the voice persisted. 'You must get up and go to the church.'

'I'll go on Saturday when I have a day off, I promise,' I replied. I wasn't even convincing to myself. I had other plans for Saturday. Five minutes later the voice spoke again. 'You have to go to the church…NOW.' And I knew that I had. Telepathy is often thought to be silent but at this time it seemed that someone was shouting in my ear down a large megaphone. Rushing down the road, just managing to catch a bus, just getting to the church on time - the local spiritualist church in the town - it couldn't be any other. Even though I wasn't a spiritualist I knew which church the voice had referred to, a picture filling my mind as the voice spoke. Sitting there with about five other people and getting nothing. No message from the 'other side' no more telepathic messages and feeling more than a little silly I sighed to myself. The presiding medium, despite the low numbers in the church, did not attempt to give me a message and at the end of the service I felt extremely confused. Then the chairperson got up to say a few words, give out notices etc and then I knew. She informed us that a psychic artist would be giving sittings at the church on the Saturday, my day off and there were a couple of vacancies. Saturday was my day off. Coincidence? Don't think so. At the close of the service I went and booked on for the Saturday reading. So that's what this was all about.

I had been asking for help over the last few months in finding out who a certain presence was, a presence that for some reason I called my Angel of God. I had felt this gentle Being around me, never coming too close but seemingly always there for over a year now. Presumably this psychic artist was going to tell me who it was. There couldn't be anything else that was urgent and required spiritual intervention.

Saturday dawned and I looked forward to my sitting. I arrived at the church and waited…and waited. Then came a message that there had been a road accident, minor, but accounting for the delay. A couple of the people waiting had to go but I was determined to stay for as long as it took. It took another two hours. The medium when he came was not alone, bringing with him two other people but as he walked through the room he gave me a very long searching look before turning left into a small room kept for the visiting medium to freshen up, have a cup of tea, compose themselves after a long journey.

I felt a little uneasy. It was as if he was seeing something unpleasant, worrying, something about me he didn't like. He was frowning as he turned away. Eventually he came to join the waiting group and began his sittings. I waited, listening with interest to three readings for this wasn't a private group. I looked at the drawings he had done whilst speaking to them, giving them messages, seeing the reactions on people's faces when they were shown their drawing. They all seemed to know the likeness, some gasping in amazement. Then it came my time for a reading. The medium began drawing and speaking at the same time, giving me information about my time in Scotland a few years earlier which was uncannily accurate even to the particular spelling of a very unusual Gaelic name which was of particular consequence to me. Then, as he continued to draw, he suddenly stopped and looked at me hard before returning to his easel. Then he smiled.

Marjorie Sutton

"There is a great deal for you to do and it isn't going to be easy. Your life will never be easy but you are very well blessed and very well protected. You are going to be working not just in this world but in others too. You have heard of the astral world?" I nodded. "Well, most of us experience coming out of our bodies at night during sleep but we don't remember. We aren't doing anything in particular so it doesn't matter. But you will remember. It will be important not just for you but in time, for others too. You will have a double life. I am not being told anymore but it will be truly amazing and it will start before too long. They want you to be prepared."

I continued to watch as he went on drawing. Well, that was a turn up for the book, the very last thing I could have expected. What on earth did it all mean? At least it should be interesting. He continued to draw, now doing a little shading, a little infilling. Who would he show me? Would he get a name? I hadn't mentioned to him that which was uppermost in my mind and he hadn't asked but by now I was curious also as to what face would appear. Would I recognise it? I hoped so. It would be most disappointing if I didn't. Then he was speaking again turning the drawing towards me.

"This is your daughter. She barely touched upon you but that little contact had to be made. Although she was your daughter, she is very highly evolved, far past anything you can imagine…and she is also… Your Angel of God."

I wanted to laugh and clap at the same time. That was amazing. The drawing brought gasps from the others still there. It was the drawing of what appeared to be a very beautiful little Indian squaw – a beautiful native American girl about eight years of age but as you looked at her eyes she matured. Years before I had had an early miscarriage. If that could come through, then the other things he had mentioned about my astral travels might also be true. I still have her picture in a frame in my healing room. 'My Angel of God.' I call her Sally after my grandmother.

When I returned home I wondered again about the strange look he had given me on his arrival. Perhaps he had seen the illness within me about to rear its head. Multiple Sclerosis was diagnosed six months later.

It hit me with all the finesse of a charging rhinoceros. I began to have bouts of blindness. I would be sitting down at home, usually in the evening or just after retiring and the room would begin to darken until every vestige of light had gone. Not only did I not see and it was very dark, I couldn't feel any part of my face or head above my nose with my hand or feel that there was anything physical there at all. No sensations, nothing. At first it was such a shock that I thought I must have fallen asleep and couldn't open my eyes but when I went to feel for my eyes I had to be very careful in case I put my finger in one of them by mistake. I couldn't feel the top of my head, my hair – nothing either by the sensation of feeling or by my physical touch.

The pain in my legs from the hips down was excruciating; rushes of energy tingling painfully down each sciatic nerve and this could last for hours. Paralysis in different parts of my body at the same time so that one part of my abdomen would feel like a ton of cold marble and a few inches away it would feel perfectly normal. Then I would be all right again for a few days but I knew that at the present rate, in a very short space of time I would be wheelchair bound.

I determined to sort my illness out. I knew without a doubt what had caused it and I believed that if I sorted out my emotions, my mental concerns and present day feelings over events that had happened a few years before, I should be able to reverse the process. So I worked hard at really looking at how the body worked. The disease was a collection of symptoms, the cause I knew and could not turn back the years or the outcomes of those years but I could work with my body in a very constructive way to bring about a full recovery. That is what I thought and I kept hold of that thought over the next two years. Immediately I started my self-healing the acute, painful symptoms went and never returned. The awful sudden bouts of blindness, one thing I had always dreaded happening to me went and never returned. The paralysis in different parts of my body went and never returned but I wasn't completely clear. The onset of MS had been severe in a very short period of time and my nervous system had been badly affected. This would take longer to repair but I knew that if I didn't give up on my body, my body wouldn't give up on me. It took another two years to really begin to get better. Sometimes the pain was bad in my legs but I worked on them all the time as I had taught myself to do and the pain lessened considerably. Sometimes when all seemed well I would suddenly feel a tingling in my face to remind me I was overdoing it and it was a very sombre reminder, which I heeded to the full.

I had had a little boy in that time much against the advice of my doctor but it was my life and I insisted in being in charge of it. My own innate healing powers played a part. My perceptions of illness are different to most peoples because I know that I can help myself and that knowledge in itself gives me a great deal of comfort. When my son was six months old he presented with an inguinal hernia, requiring an operation. I gave him healing one night and despite me being ill, the hernia never presented again. When six months later he was called to the hospital for surgery, I wavered. A hernia could strangulate. I couldn't risk what I couldn't see. Despite my beliefs I had to take into account the feelings of my husband who was leaving the decision up to myself. The child looked and behaved fine. There didn't appear to be a problem at all but I was unsure. What if I was wrong. He could die. I rang the doctor and made arrangements for him to have the operation. I felt extremely guilty as I saw my son being wheeled into theatre smiling and waving to me with his favourite bear in hand.

After the operation, the surgeon came into our room where he lay recovering and informed me that although he had operated, the hernia had already been healed and the scar tissue was there to prove it. He said he thought I knew something about this and he thought that his news would put my mind at rest. Then he turned on his heels and walked out of the room. He was a young man from New Zealand on an exchange visit it seemed. Lucky for me he was in theatre that morning. An English doctor would not have behaved in that way and I would never have known the amazing ability a baby or child has to be healed so quickly. From then on I knew that I would never doubt again what had been healed, whether I could see it or not. And I never have. I didn't know it then but shortly after this my spiritual work in other dimensions would set up again. And how.

Dress Rehearsal

It all began after a particularly uneventful day. I had gone to bed early to read a book. Book reading had always been relegated to bedtimes since my teenage years. Then it had been my only escape from unpleasant scenes that had occurred between my parents from time to time. My father was great on mental abuse. Years later, I found that I never had time to read during the day and because I enjoyed it so much, it became a luxury, a 'get away from it all' treat in the late evening. I fell asleep with no warning or premonition of what was to follow but I had been somewhere with my grandparents who had by now both died. That had been very vivid. I had had no truly spiritual experiences outside of healing, since my teenage years and so was not really prepared for the re awakening of the spiritual side of my life despite the prophecy from the psychic artist eighteen months before.

I awoke feeling rather strange and I became aware of my own bedroom and the sleeping figure of my husband silhouetted against the light shining in through the bedroom window, courtesy of a kindly lamppost. I was very conscious of my immediate surroundings, my pillows for example and the knowledge that I was back in this world but the feeling I had known within the other world was still there and getting stronger all the time. It was as if before I went any further I had to have the reassurance that I was still alive in this world, at this time. Normality, reality was back. That seemed to be the message. But everything was not normal. I wasn't, and I knew that I was going to come completely out of my body. In a flash, my mind flitted back to that time eighteen months before. I recalled how I had seen the medium who had told me of how I would journey to the astral dimensions and that I would remember it. That I would have an amazing life, not least in other worlds. At the time, although I understood what he was saying, I hadn't for some reason expected that when it happened that it would happen like this. I wasn't too worried. I just wanted someone to know where I was going, what was happening to me. How long would it take and would I be back in time for breakfast? I am nothing if not a practical lady. I didn't want anyone thinking I had died or was suffering from some awful disease because they couldn't waken me. I wasn't to know at this stage how everything was going to work.

I tried to put my hand out to my husband but could not move. It became imperative to me to have someone hold my hand and I tried to awaken my husband and tell him what was happening but even as I willed it with all my might, I knew that it was hopeless. Although my mouth tried to speak the words and the words were clear in my head, he couldn't hear because I wasn't speaking in this dimension. I remember thinking to myself that in many instances when people were in coma or deeply unconscious, words were spoken by them but we heard nothing. Lips could not move to make a sound that could not be heard although the intelligence within was fully alert. They had passed the barrier that separates us from other dimensions, other worlds and before slipping away myself, I realised that trying to cry out was a fruitless exercise. I was in this on my own. How could it be otherwise.

Slipping away, is not the correct expression. Going with a bang was much more like it. There was a sudden hard tug at my solar plexus and at the same time it felt as if my head had been axed from my body. Immediately, I was out of my body in the darkness. I could see nothing. I felt rather like a genie coming out of the lamp, expanding to my normal size until I was completely out and then I felt normal except that I couldn't see. It had all happened so quickly and here I was, out of body. What would happen next, where would I go?

I was completely aware of myself as being virtually the same as when I inhabited a physical body although I felt a lot lighter, a certain lack of weight but not quite a sense of weightlessness. There was no heaviness just a feeling of freedom. That other place, that other body was of no consequence to me now. Hovering above the bed I presumed, I tried to prise my eyes open for a time, first by raising my eyebrows and trying to raise my eyelids and then gently trying with my fingers before remembering that as my eyes were not physical, they would not 'open'. Instead I would just have to will my vision to see. Sure enough, as I put my mind to it, the mind being the clue to everything, the blackness turned to a lightening grey, rather like a blind coming slowly down and taking the darkness with it, and then I could see properly again. I had to smile to myself. I had become so enmeshed in the physical I seemed to have forgotten what once had been so natural to me.

It was still dark in the bedroom, which surprised me. It was just as if nothing really had changed in many ways. For some reason I had expected it to be as light as day for me because I wasn't in that dimension but of course in a way I was. I had only stepped out of my body. No one would be able to see me who was still enmeshed in a physical field but I would be able to see them and myself, lying there. I still waited for the brightness to appear, but it didn't and I realised that this was it. I marvelled at what an amateur I was. In a few short years I had forgotten just how it was being out of body. I was surrounded by a grey darkness whether in one body or another.

I was still in the bedroom and my first thought was that I did not want to see myself lying there on the bed. I'm not sure why but the feeling was very strong. I repeated over and over again to whoever might be listening, probably myself, that I definitely didn't want to look down and see myself. And I didn't. In fact I didn't see the bed at all or the light coming in through the partly open curtains. As I began to look around to reassure myself that I was still in my bedroom, I began to move quickly, from wall to wall, back and forth, back and forth like someone on the end of an elastic band. Each time I tried to stop and slow down, the awareness of the walls surrounding me pulled me back. After quite a period of time I asked that 'it' stopped. I hadn't expected this, didn't know what was happening and I was becoming exhausted. After what felt like a blip, I fell to the floor at the side of the bed. I lay there in a crumpled mess breathing out hard. Surely it was all supposed to be so effortless.

I thought back to the strange elastic bouncing and no sooner had I thought it, then I was off again. I recall vividly the feeling of great tiredness as I flew rapidly back and forth, screwing myself up into a ball as I crashed into the walls. But the walls were like barriers of cotton wool and I was not hurt. They slowed my progress but only minimally as I flew across the room and I was feeling so tired. Why would that be? What on earth was all this about I wondered. Then I asked for help and protection, still seeking for a hand to hold for reassurance. I wasn't afraid but I was unsure of what would happen next. I desperately needed someone to explain to me, what I was experiencing. Why I was flying across the room; why I wasn't going anywhere. Is this all there was? Surely not.

Far from being in awe of what was happening to me, I was still a very practical lady. I needed to know all the whys and wherefores of every situation, in this realm or any other and this particular experience was beginning to bug me. Everything had to have a meaning. Experiences were meant to illuminate and educate, not leave one wondering. What happened next was that a hand took hold of mine. My right hand. It was a big hand, warm and firm and oh, so comforting.

'Thank you,' I breathed. 'Thank you.' The next moment another person took hold of my left hand. I was standing upright now facing the bedroom wall at the foot of the bed. The wall had disappeared and because I was in my astral body I could be and see at the same time. The bedroom wall disappeared and I watched me walk away between two very tall beings, as if I was a child again taking a walk with two adults not exactly down a tunnel but as if I was on a woodland path. There was a sense of direction here. It felt so wonderful, so safe, and so beautiful. I would have gone anywhere with them without a thought for the physical plane. It was still there but for me it no longer existed. I joined the little trio and became one with myself again, part of the experience. Not just a spectator.

Almost immediately I found myself in another bedroom in a cottage we had once rented. I was being shown around but no one spoke and so I did not know what it was all about. I still couldn't see who was with me there was just a feeling of someone close by. It was much lighter and I could see very plainly. This was a scene that was half true. I recognised pieces of furniture we had rented along with the cottage but other scenes, seemed to be imposed in an effort to tell me something. I repeatedly asked. "What am I to make of this. What are you trying to show me?" But whoever was with me did not speak, even telepathically. Or perhaps I was just rusty. I knew I was with just one presence now, a male influence but who, I knew not and the reason for it I knew not. I saw my family in bed, wide awake, excited but at what I knew not. No one was speaking. Again it was like watching a silent movie. It wasn't a scene that had ever actually taken place and as my children were older now, I was lost as to what I was supposed to understand by it. Years later it was made plain to me by subsequent events but at that time, such an explanation was not credible even with my imagination.

Eventually, I spoke to my companion and asked that I may return. I felt absolutely exhausted. I had used up so much energy in my own bedroom before my release that it was now telling on me. I thanked this most gentle of creatures whose presence was so strong, apologising for my weakness, explaining that I was too tired to interpret what I was being shown. Immediately, I found myself back in body, in my own bed, wide awake. My husband had not moved, nothing had altered in that room, only my life had altered yet again and I knew that this was only the beginning.

It was a long time before I could get back to sleep. I wondered who had come to my aid and guided me to that other house and why. Why? That was the big question. Following on that was the question I was to ask repeatedly for over two years. Why had I been unable to get out of my bedroom on my own. The physical walls had not stopped me. In effect there were no walls and why should it tire my astral body. It didn't make any sense to me. The next day I went to work as usual. That night as I lay in bed, reading, it suddenly came into my mind, that I may have a similar experience tonight too. I shrugged it off and switched off the light. The tugging at my solar plexus at once began again and I sat up in bed. "No. No, not tonight please. I have to come to terms with what happened last night. Please do not come for me again until I am ready." The tugging did not come again and I slept soundly.

In the following weeks I thought about my nocturnal journey. What I had seen, was I believed symbolic, but what it symbolised I could not tell. It was all a mystery to me. A lot of effort had gone into the exercise, it couldn't have been for nothing. Why was I being particularly dense? Somebody, somewhere wanted me to know something. Was something wrong now? Was I being prepared for something? As always, deep inside I knew that I would have to work it out for myself. Would *they* come back for me? And who were *they*? My beloved grandmother had been the first to help me, that feeling had been very strong, but afterwards, another accompanied that presence, a male influence and not someone I had met in this incarnation. It was a puzzle and one that would take me years to resolve to my satisfaction.

Shortly after this I became pregnant. There would be no more adventures for a little while. I needed all my energies to meet the needs of the incoming spirit, which would take the form of a boy child, a very special child in terms of spiritual growth whose host, or mother had to be spiritually aware. Someone who would provide the right vibrations at the right time. Someone who would be there to guide and understand. Someone who would listen when he was young and who would help as he grew into manhood. Someone who would help him to grasp the opportunity. Someone who would be there to support the very difficult growth of the advanced spirit on this heavy physical plane.

After the birth of my son it was some time before I considered the spiritual work that I had to do. I was still recovering from Multiple Sclerosis and my time was taken up by this new arrival. I was however to have a particular question answered and in order for this to be done properly I did experience leaving my body and returning to it very slowly, yet fully conscious.

Being a practical person with a nursing background, I often wondered what happened to the physical body when the astral body had left. As always I had asked over a period of time to be shown how it felt and as always at the appropriate time the answer was given. First of all, I knew that the spirit, the intelligence within, often took a respite from this earthly load by venturing out but that for most people they never remembered where they went. Most didn't actually go anywhere but drifted above the body as a boat might drift at its moorings as the current moved it.

Most people didn't even recognise that they may do this as a natural occurrence. What I needed to know, was the effect on the body when the spirit was absent and I spent much time reflecting upon the subject. Did it become agitated, restless or did it become lifeless almost, the energy fields no longer surrounding it for a time.

This particular night I must have been out a little while perhaps just drifting and it was only when I was to return to my body that I became aware. I had just entered the physical and had not yet 'clicked' in. I realised that as I was returning to body, my bedroom began to take shape around me and my body was lying just beneath my awareness.

My first impression was the noise. It was terrific, like being in the bowels of a large ship. I could hardly cope with the noise that assailed me. There was a loud creaking as might be heard on a ship and a particular churning sensation and sounds like I have never before heard. At first I wondered what was happening to my house, as it seemed to come from outside of me as if I could hear all this with my physical ears. I probably could as I was just entering my body but it took a few seconds to realise that the sounds were coming from *inside* my body. They were much louder than the normal sounds of a stomach gurgling or wind whistling through the bowel. The churning of the engines, were of course the workings of my digestive system. The creaking was unbelievable. It was difficult at first to discern where the sounds were indeed coming from as I was aware of the physical room around me. As I concentrated I realised that I was listening to the machinations of twenty odd feet of bowel not to mention the non stop work the liver and kidneys do and the stomach. I lay listening to the gentle slurp of the liquids in their containers, the gall bladder, the stomach, the bladder; pictures of each of these organs appearing in my mind in graphic sequence. For a little while I just lay there and marvelled. Then there was a noise like the rushing of the wind. I wanted to cover my ears to stop the drums from bursting. It was all around me, like standing on the top of a mountain in a gale at the same time recognising the ebb and flow of it. I realised that this was my breathing and after listening in amazement for some time, I took the opportunity to count the respirations. Despite my own excitement at being able to carry out this minor analysis, counting was a slow process meaning that the number of respirations were perfectly normal for someone resting. Next came the sound of an express train racing through my body. I knew immediately that this was the blood racing around the blood system and just like a train it passed over the lines, corresponding to blood in the veins passing over the bones which produce the pulses. That too was normal for someone at rest but again it was so terribly loud.

I was able to take my time and monitor everything two or three times to ensure that the readings I got were true. I just felt that I was wandering around my body, exploring, listening to the roars and the rumbles of a wonderful machine at work. The image was again of the bowels of the engine room perhaps of a great liner. I imagined the darkness and stokers hard at work to keep the energies burning whilst listening to things I don't believe anyone could ever hear, except in this way. It took me by surprise. The noise was unbelievable. Did a baby hear this dreadful noise continuously. No, I believe the womb protects it from the sound of its mother's machine-like noise but it possibly hears the sounds relating to itself but faintly as it is in a watery environment. Then as I accepted what I was being shown, I slowly 'clicked' in, sounds fading away… and everything was back to normal.

It had been a wonderful, amazing experience that was over all too soon. I lay there and ran my fingers over my skin. There was no hint of perspiration, nothing to suggest that I had felt such excitement. My physical body was under perfct control. I thanked them most profusely. What an amazing experience. One that I have never experienced again but then you only need such an experience once in any lifetime.

It would be some time before I was to understand why I had had such difficulty in getting out of my bedroom that first time but as always, the question *was* eventually answered. I arrived home from work one evening and sat in front of the fireplace which was situated in a large expanse of wall. As I rested and stared at this wall I suddenly knew. The reason I couldn't get out of the bedroom was because I hadn't tried to. If I had seen myself *leaving* the bedroom, I would have done so immediately. Instead I had kept seeing the bedroom walls in my minds eye and in so doing I had kept them there. The power of the mind. As we think, so we are. It brought home to me too how we keep ourselves static in our own little worlds when just knowing we can do something will make it happen. It is all in the knowing. Instead of visualising negatives things surrounding us in our lives we should only dwell on the positive for what we think we can truly bring about. As always it was just too simple.

Night School On The Astral Plane

Being spiritually aware since birth, my reawakening in adulthood to spiritual values and structures made me eager to spend my time when it was appropriate in those other dimensions, on those other planes, reuniting from time to time with those I held in high esteem. I did however realise there was still much for me to learn, or re learn, opening again those doors to my mind that would bring true knowledge and memories flooding back into my present consciousness.

In the seventies I was very much concerned about brain damaged babies and was working in a voluntary capacity following a programme that became known as Philadelphia Patterning. This involved teams of six or eight people working with a brain damaged baby in such a way as to encourage other brain cells to take over from the damaged cells. It was a heavy programme of exercises, repeated throughout the day to stimulate growth and to stimulate good brain cells to take over from the damaged tissues. It was proving to be successful with some children making excellent progress mentally and physically. It was however time consuming, we sometimes worked as a team for eight hours at a time with one child and many exercises had to be continued for life. The benefits this programme brought about were enough to convince loved ones that it was all worth while but I often pondered on a simpler way. For me there had to be more than what we were doing. More and simpler. Man had to discover more about how the brain worked. We knew nothing about vast areas of the brain and I was sure the secret of repair was in there somewhere. I had been particularly concerned about young people with cerebral palsy since I had first encountered a young girl with this condition shortly after I began my training as a nurse.

One day I had received a patient with cerebral palsy onto the ward due to having broken both her legs. I was instructed to 'special' her – meaning that I should be responsible for her primarily, on the ward. I think there was some concern as to how she had broken both legs and perhaps the authorities wanted to know if she was in fact not being cared for adequately. She wasn't exactly petite but only a slight thing not weighing very much at all. Making eye contact was impossible it seemed as her eyes rolled from side to side when open and her mouth could utter only screams and other strange sounds. I felt at a loss as to how to communicate to her. The attitude at that time was that she wouldn't know anything, her brain would be very damaged and all that we could do would be to care for her physical needs to the best of our ability.

After a couple of days, whenever I was washing her or making her bed, I would tell her all the little tit bits of the ward. Which doctor fancied which nurse, the silly things that new nurses on the ward did, anything remotely of interest I had done before, trying to be witty and interesting. Perhaps I thought something would go in. Two weeks after she was admitted her mother and her sister arrived to visit her. Apparently they lived many miles away and couldn't get there more regularly. I kept out of the way but watched their behaviour towards her. There were many kisses and much hugging- carefully- and holding of hands. Both focussed on her entirely during that hour, apparently laughing and listening and holding just the sort of animated conversation anyone might make, punctuated by screams from the bed. Would she understand them I thought, after all they were close and seemed such a loving family. When it came time for them to leave, they sought me out. 'Nurse Robinson, we can't thank you enough for looking after Denise. She has had us in stitches listening to her tales of life here, especially all the things you bother to tell her'.

What sort of things?' I asked, wondering what on earth they were talking about. 'You know, about so and so and so and so'. I nearly died. 'It was just a bit of fun' I said weakly.

'You didn't know she could understand you did you?' They laughed again. 'You have a wonderful sense of humour and Denise loves a sense of humour. She really misses you when you are off. I believe you are going to see......' And so it went on. Apparently they had worked hard since her birth to communicate with her and they had certainly done so brilliantly as far as I was concerned. I didn't have the time to ask them. Perhaps her hearing was better than we believed possible or telepathy on her part probably and they understood the type of sounds she emitted, had it all down to a fine art.

When the last of the visitors had gone and it was time for me to attend once more to Denise, I went over to her bed and looked down at her. I willed her to look at me and for a few moments, her eyes stopped their restless movements and looked back at me. Deep inside there was a very beautiful woman. It was like looking into her very soul. All the intelligence in the world lay inside that little frame. Then her eyes were moving again and cries were coming from her mouth. 'You gave all my little secrets away Denise. For that I'm going to tickle you till you scream for mercy.' Screaming set up at once and I smiled at her. 'You don't give much away do you?' I said.

After that I told her everything that I could, read the newspapers to her, discussed the local and national news and was terribly upset when it was time for her to return to her home. She in turn thanked me through her mother for making her hospital visit such fun.

Now of course we realise that there is an intelligence inside each cerebral palsy person, computers especially bringing him or her into contact with others like nothing before has managed to. All I could think of then was the suffering and anguish which must go on inside those little heads when everyone ignored them and treated them like so much vegetation. I wanted so badly to know what could be done. There was so much brain tissue of which we knew nothing and Philadelphia Patterning seemed to have some of the answers. I joined a team working for six hours or so once a week. The teams worked months at a time and the children undergoing patterning had to keep the exercises up for life, perhaps a small price for seeing and hearing again but how wonderful it would be if we knew how to do a complete reversal which would simply AutoCorrect.

One night I simply went to sleep as usual and found myself out of body outside a large imposing building with wide steps leading up to a large open entrance. Columns reached from the floor upwards to a ceiling I could not see. Large poster and notice boards were dotted around advertising various events and as I reached the top of the steps I could see there were many people milling around looking for some particular subject perhaps or just looking. Some were standing around making notes as they wandered from one board to another. As I got closer and went on my own little tour, I could see that frames held television type monitors; computers as we now know them had not arrived on earth at this stage. Large notice boards advertising different subjects dominated certain areas of this immense open space, directing people to the various subjects they could view on these monitors. As I continued to make my way around I began to think of what I would like to learn. It seemed to be some sort of university but when I thought of this, another thought entered my head. 'These are the Halls of Learning'. Telepathy at play immediately. I had heard of this title from a spiritualist book read years before and my first thought was… So, they are right about this at least. As always in my sojourn out of body to other planes or in other dimensions I was to find a particular lack of colour. It was like being in a black and white movie. There were hundreds of people milling around, some seeming to know what they were looking for, and others looking about them in surprise. Eventually I made my way across to where a large crowd was gathered around one of the screens. **Brain damage** was written across the screen.

Aha. Now this should be wonderfully interesting. As I became absorbed in the subject my awareness of others being around me left and I felt myself to be alone as I stared up at the screen. A formula was being written. I had never heard of a formula for brain damage but then I wasn't a scientist or a physicist. Who knew at what level these very clever people worked. I stared at the figures displayed. The story of brain damage was relayed in this way and just as I was wondering what all the figures actually meant, again I was told telepathically to watch the screen. Sure enough two of the figures on one side of the equation were reversed. That was the answer to brain damage. I stood there in shock. It was so simple. I stood looking up at the screen for a long time, extremely excited. I would find a scientist who would understand these figures and the equation and they would be able to correct brain damage – at birth – before birth? It was so exciting. I began a chanting in my head, thank you, thank you and thank you.

I immediately found myself wide awake back in bed. I got up to make a cup of tea, the figures dancing in my head. It was so simple. It was wonderful. It might take some time, but surely somebody somewhere would listen to me and try it. I walked about for over an hour, marvelling at what I had been shown, what this could do for the world. Where should I start? Who should I write to? I really didn't have a clue. Having worked within nursing and the medical community I was fully aware that it wouldn't be easy. How do you go up to a consultant neurologist and say 'Oh bye the way, I have the answer to brain damage?' Still terribly excited I lay down and eventually dropped off to sleep again.

Over the next few days I couldn't keep my mind off this wonderful discovery. Then disaster struck. I woke up one morning and I could not remember the formulae. It had I thought been imprinted on my mind forever - and it was gone. It was unbelievable. I was distraught. To have been shown that and to have lost it! Why hadn't I written it down! It had been so simple that's why. I never thought I could have possibly forgotten it but I had. Despite all my pleas to be shown again, I never have been.

For a time I consoled myself with the knowledge that I had never heard of a formulae or equation for brain injury so perhaps the knowledge would have been to no avail. It was before its time and when the time was right it would be given to me again. Perhaps I had simply been shown the future and giving this message to mankind had not been my responsibility after all. Perhaps I was being given a glimpse of the future. Perhaps someone I had not yet met was working away on this and when the time was right, would incarnate and bring it to the world. Then why show me the answer? I still believe that I was in some way involved but didn't get it right. It was certainly a learning experience for me. About twenty years after this happened, I was sitting in some waiting area, thumbing through a magazine when there it was. Not the answer but the equation. A number of them to be precise. None of them rang any bells but here we were, using equations to quantify brain damage. Back came the old desperation. I had failed miserably. As there hasn't been a treatment for brain damage I can only assume that the large crowd around that particular monitor had also failed or been unable to bring the message back to this plane for whatever reason. I still think of this and shudder at my stupidity. I just hadn't been up to the job.

Marjorie Sutton

In my role as a healer I have dealt successfully with brain damage in the tiny baby but wonderful as that is, it hasn't taught mankind how to deal with correcting brain damage on the larger scale which also presupposes a greater knowledge of the brain itself than we have at present. It was to be a year or so before I returned to the halls of learning and this time I found myself in the 'reading room' where I was given a desk and a pile of papers to read. It really was what I imagined a very large university library to be like, with probably hundreds of tables and thousands of books. Large windows took up most of the walls, which looked old, and a natural light entered. There were no shadows in that room and I felt that there were many other rooms very similar to this one just out of my vision. I was expected and the material I had to study was placed before me in a very efficient no nonsense way. No 'How are you today, or Hi, what's it like down there these days?'

The reading material was very similar to our newspapers which I read from cover to cover. There was no let up. When I finished one another appeared beneath until I was so tired and exhausted that I asked if I could return to body. Another paper was placed in front of me and I began again. I had a feeling of boredom rather than excitement. It seemed that I was just absorbing knowledge for the sake of it, over and over again. Eventually I was allowed to go but told that in future when I arrived I must come straight to this room again and continue from the particular column of papers, that would be waiting for me on my table. Time and time again I returned to this room to re read the same papers despite my protestations of knowledge at what they contained. I was told very firmly to stop moaning and read on; that I had to continue absorbing this information until given permission to stop. It all seemed a waste of time as wearily I would sit and begin my nightly reading sessions. Unless I needed to ask a question, my mentor kept her distance. Sometimes I just saw hands placing the piles in front of me that gave me an impression of male or female, mostly female.

I now realise that I was being taught a great deal about healing and about people. The two of course have to be connected. Illness doesn't just arrive although it gives every appearance of doing just that and it doesn't always stay just for the sake of it. I learned the correlation between thought and body, how the body was programmed to deal with any problems it encountered. The relationship between the emotional and mental aspects acting on the physical. The overall importance of energy fields, not just our own but other people's and those of the Earth itself. How these could precipitate illness in some cases and how they played a vital part in keeping us safe within our own space; safe from other stronger energies both from the earth plane and other dimensions. Later I was to realise that here was the source of my inherent knowledge, a knowledge that had helped me to overcome Multiple Sclerosis and the onset of Cancer. A knowledge I could teach to others.

Marjorie Sutton

In some measure I was also being shown the future so that when certain events took place in my life, I never questioned, became upset or rebelled but simply got on with the work and my life. I discovered too that there had been much to prepare me for in my life here. Meeting and dealing with certain people has been very important in the scheme of things. People who I had to teach who eventually came into my life that I recognised had to be dealt with. I had been shown the unfolding of things that I promptly forgot until the people appeared in my life and whom I then tried my best to help. Without that prior knowledge I probably wouldn't have allowed myself to get involved but it was important for their and probably my karma or destiny.

Sometimes I believe it has been like reading the script of a play. My Play. Horrible things have happened and I have known that ...this. is... just... part of the script. Play your part as best you can that is all that you can do... even to the point of sighing with relief when someone has left my life despite me loving them very much. I haven't escaped any of the pain or the misery that life throws up and at least I know I did my best even if it doesn't always look like that.

The halls of learning also deal with advice and there has been overwhelming help for me from those who seem to be an integral part of my physical life, albeit from elsewhere. They have really tried so hard to keep the show on the road until all avenues have been explored by all of us, including the ones who wanted to opt out of the 'play'. Unfortunately, for me, the loved ones I spent time with from this world, trying to sort things out there, on the astral could never remember these experiences which would have made life a great deal simpler. Or at least they said they didn't and I do believe them. This world is so confining and it is so easy to go astray for fame or fortune or simply because people get tired of it all here. But Life is truly an obstacle race and the more fun you have getting over the obstacles the better it will be but so many just get too embroiled. They take life all too seriously, making mountains out of molehills or hiding their heads in the sand looking for easy options.

Help and information is only given in this way, in the Halls of Learning when situations are extremely important and they have given me added insight into the machinations of life on and around earth. Never ever stop believing that somebody up there loves you - ALL the time no matter how it seems here. One can receive help here when dealing with relationship problems that threaten to disorganise the on-going Play but just like on earth people have to want to go down a certain path, stay in a certain relationship in order for the Play to come to its ultimate conclusion. When on the astral level people do recognise the earth life for what it is and promise to do what needs to be done, knowing that time there is short but once back in body it isn't always that easy. Too often the Play has to be abandoned or a redirection has to occur and the remaining players are left in a kind of limbo.

Marjorie Sutton

There is a difference however between honouring your commitments made pre-life and staying with a person or in a situation which is long past its sell by date. There are times when people have to move on, meet other people when present karma has been fulfilled. Sometimes death brings things to a halt, other times people just walk away, that particular experience over and both parties can meet those they were destined to meet or do the job they were destined to do a little later in life. If certain things have to happen or certain people have to meet, it will be brought about. People elsewhere will pull out all the stops to ensure you each fulfil your destiny. We see this when people have remarkable escapes from accidents or appear to just get lucky being in the right place at the right time. Nothing happens by chance if by that happening something remarkable occurs.

Sometimes in the Halls one catches a glimpse of an earthly acquaintance in a heated discussion with their mentor, obviously not too happy with something, not accepting what they are actually being shown. In this sphere the camera doesn't lie and eventually the people have to return, still mumbling to themselves something about life not being fair! The halls of learning are just that and many, many people spend much time there over many years. Do you ever have cause to think to yourself, 'Now where did that thought come from? How did I know…?' Perhaps this is the answer. Certainly, any true desire by you to learn more about spiritual matters will trigger a response sooner or later if it is appropriate for you to know. If you have a particular question to ask, ask every night before you go to sleep and eventually you will get the answer and if you wake up in the middle of the night shouting 'Eureka' for goodness sake WRITE IT DOWN.

An Irish Connection

I had visited Northern Ireland the year before the later hostilities which were to last over 30 years broke out. I had hired a car and toured around the area staying at hotels, guest houses and farms in that green and pleasant land. Everywhere there was peace and tranquility, a stepping back in time almost to a way of life only found now in the remoter villages of England. The people were funny in a nice way. One could make the mistake of thinking they were particularly obsequious, touching their forelock or their cap in greeting but this was simply their way. In England we speak of people being 'Irish' meaning doing the obviously wrong thing, being illogical or just not making sense but in an affectionate way. They are definitely different to the more mongrel of the mainland species. They can be very superstitious and very warm hearted and make you rock with laughter, seemingly happy to laugh at themselves. It is their way of making you feel OK. One could be forgiven for thinking there was just a little missing 'upstairs' sometimes but these people never missed a thing. Behind the banter there can be a very astute mind at work.

So it was that when I found myself, out of body in Ireland, in Belfast, I thought how very sad it was that so many atrocities were being committed in such a beautiful land. I didn't recognise it from its buildings but from its vibration. There is a peculiarly damp vibration when betrayal plays a major role in people's lives. Surely there has to be a great deal of betrayal during a civil war.

I was entering a public house where there was to be a wedding reception. The centre of the floor had been cleared for dancing and tables set around the sides. As I stood by the bar and looked around the room I wondered just how secure I was. Waiting until people were seated, enjoying their drinks and chatting away as one does on these occasions, I moved in to where a woman was sat between two men and, in my astral body, I went close and sat on her knee. A lot of drink can open up the auric field just as many drugs can and I was able to get very close. I waited, chuckling to myself, feeling quite wicked, hoping that she would pick up on me. I wasn't to find out for someone gave me a very quick reminder that I was here to work, not play, chiding me for my flippancy at such a time.

I quickly moved away, apologised to whoever might be listening and the lady whose space I had invaded and got on with the work.

This took the form of me scrutinising everyone who came into the room, looking for the one who would betray their hosts. The room quickly filled up and the celebrations got under way.

It seemed to me as evening approached, one would be made clear to me who, although taking of the hospitality of the family, would, when the time was right, leave their package of despair and walk away. It was my job to try to stop them or failing that to try to alert someone to the danger that was in their midst. I looked about me to see if any other help was at hand from my present dimension but there were no astral forms. I was aware that there is always help at hand, that requests or prayers are always heard and, all things being equal, answered and I wasn't at all worried or concerned about my safety. It was simply a matter of interest to me of who might be there and would it be anyone I knew. I would do my best in my role and I was sure that others would be working hard in theirs.

I watched as the young newly weds arrived and were greeted and feted, starting the dancing as evening approached. They then left, no doubt for their honeymoon as did some of the guests who later reappeared with others to continue the celebrations into the night. Time is essentially speeded up for me in these situations so that whilst time did not hang or drag whilst I waited around there were small lulls in the proceedings.

It was as the room became a little less crowded that I saw and recognised him. An old man wearing a cloth cap and smoking a pipe sat at a table finishing his drink. I had noticed him at the outset sitting at a large table with others and I was appalled. I had expected a young man, an intruder, a gatecrasher perhaps but not an invited guest as indeed this old man was.

I watched as he now supped on his own, the dancing for the time being delayed for those who had left the room to find refreshments. I felt sick and angry, disgusted that one who should have been encouraging restraint to younger, hotter heads was a key player. Certainly one who no one would remotely suspect of betrayal and the taking of life.

I looked carefully again around the room. There were no packages with their deadly message but there would be, he would see to that. When he arose he nodded to those nearby, before leaving the public house. I followed him to where he went to telephone the assassin. I had not been mistaken. I metaphorically shivered as I continued to follow down the street where hours before a young couple had been so happy on their special day, never thinking for one minute they had a traitor in their midst. As he made his dreadful journey of hate I tried telepathically to appeal to his sense of reason. I tried to affect his conscience but he was hell bent on being the good party member, the link in the chain of destruction, which was at this time still in its early days on the physical plane.

The man returned later with a young man in tow. I still did not know or see my co workers but always there are others who work, separately or in groups. That night much work was done by these unseen helpers to stop the carnage. It was not completely successful but there was no loss of life. The damage had been limited.

I returned to physical consciousness with the horror of betrayal pervading my being and to this day I can feel the sick vibrations of that unhappy island whenever I think of the work I did there over a period of four or five years in the late seventies and early eighties. The only time that I returned to physical consciousness with fear embracing me was after a rescue mission again in Northern Ireland.

This time I was working with a blonde woman, who I seem to recollect, was called Betty. I didn't know her in the physical world but she was a visible co worker in the next dimension. We had the task of trying to stop two men planting a terrible bomb. This is a prime example of how *all people* can operate in other dimensions.

One is not always dealing with those on the physical plane from an astral or other dimension. Sometimes one has to work with others who also work within the astral or other dimensions in order to get closer to them. In other words, we sometimes have to work with those others who are also out of body. This particular night I was engaged in such work with Betty. We met in a meeting room where our two objectives would be. As soon as we recognised them we realised the extent of their sense of purpose. I could not say with all honesty which organisation they belonged to but their aims were to maim and kill. They were key players at the time for their organisation and it was our job to try to get them to rethink their strategy. One cannot be for or against any particular party or organisation. It is a recognised fact that people do what they think is right in their eyes and in the Northern Ireland situation there is much hatred and bitterness fanned by the flames of fanaticism by those whose need for revenge is strong. All we could attempt was compromise. If we could just influence them enough for them to stop and think on this occasion, affect their hearts, who knew what it might lead to.

Being in another dimension does not make individuals into super human beings capable of magic. Many things have to be taken into account. Personal responsibility is still uppermost. Karma has a definite role to play but not always in the way it is perceived on earth. But just as others were trying to resolve the problem in this country by talking, we were attempting to help by getting closer into the emotional fields and mental fields of these key players. We all create the future day by day. The old saying that 'tomorrow never comes' is true. We must learn from the past and live the moment and in this way, the decision taken NOW will create the future for us. It was our task to influence the NOW if we could. With these people, we soon realised that they were involved in astral work and that they did their espionage work in this way. I don't know if they recalled what had happened after they had returned to their physical bodies but the knowledge gained whilst they were operating on an astral level would remain with them, taking the form of hunches and intuition, which in turn made them very successful.

The time arrived when we all met in the astral sphere and we chatted and discussed many things but nothing to do with the Irish situation. We did not disclose our true roles to them, as they would have rejected us as they would in the physical sphere. We agreed to meet them again and this we did on a number of occasions when eventually they told us of their future intent. We tried to persuade them of the cycle of destruction they were setting up in a situation where no one could win and many innocent victims could die, families left bereft for life but for them, the 'cause' was greater than life itself.

They had to take a journey on the physical level in order to create mayhem and Betty and I joined them in astral consciousness. They were unaware of our presence for most of the journey as we tried so hard to create the thought forms which might just give them a change of heart. To our dismay, before the journey was completed, they picked up on us and the hatred focused for so long on their chosen objective turned on us.

We knew that we had to abandon this mission. On return to the physical consciousness I was sweating with the emotion of fear. The only time this had ever happened to me. They were very dangerous men - in any dimension. That feeling stayed with me for hours and I realised perhaps for the first time the danger in which I could find myself, in other dimensions. A very good reason for practicing auricl 'washes' frequently. Every day, morning and evening, I thank the Father for His protection knowing too that I must play my part.

I have never knowingly been involved in such a mission in that country again. However, it brought it home to me that what I could do for good, another could do for bad, which brought up a great many questions about 'haunted' houses and mediumship. It also hammered home to me what I already knew but perhaps needed reinforcement of, the statement, 'the intention is all'.

I spent many hours speculating on how much work is done in other dimensions by the living. Usually people have talked about the help possible from those who have left the physical through death and about the negative work done that can be done after death. Therefore this was a new, very broad area for me to consider and again it begged many more questions that I had never considered before. The experiences in Northern Ireland made me look at the concept of the 'haunted house'. People always assume that some earth bound spirit dwells there, making its presence known from time to time by knockings or smells or strange sensations experienced by those around. There is little to say that the spirit is from another world as it may be just be someone out of body, somebody who doesn't even remember it. Could this be the real reason for déjà vu? And is every 'presence' that of a person who has died? Or is it someone out of body? I think it is worth begging the question. Some people report how they were helped by another who they could not see but who spoke to them, who got them out of a hole, or how they just 'knew' what to do instinctively. This helper doesn't have to be from another world but somebody very much from this just putting in a little bit of overtime here.

We shouldn't be afraid, we should be questioning any strange experience. We should never stop learning about our true Selves for by doing this we begin to learn just a little more about our Creator and if that isn't worth doing I don't know what is.

Call of Africa

I was out again but this time with a difference. And what a difference! At first, as I gazed around me at the immediate scene below I was unaware that much was different. It was only as I looked further afield and seemingly around on myself, that I realised that the difference was within me. *I was without form.* No hands, legs, body, head, nothing physical or astral or relating to form at all. Just an intelligence, which could see, comprehend and move.

I was still *me,* the essential me, still feeling that my awareness was still in that place behind my eyes, where it usually sits, no more or less intelligent than I normally am but I had no body. Strange, very strange, but novel. Then I remembered vividly my arrival on the earth plane. That short space of time before I had been drawn into my present life form had been the same. I had 'stood' and watched as my future family went about its daily business. I *was* and I *was* simply *there.*

Marjorie Sutton

I quickly realised that I must be inhabiting my mental energy system or 'body' because all I needed to do was think- and see. Think about what I was seeing, where I was and why I was where I was. I couldn't hear anything or feel any other sensations normally attributable to the physical form, like touch or smell or feel heat and cold but I could somehow see in the normal manner for someone out of body around the physical plane

As I continued to look around me I realised that I was airborne, moving, somewhere over Africa, the Congo to be precise. Not having ever been to Africa I did question if my first assumption had been correct. I was assured telepathically that it was. This presupposes that there was someone else there with me but it was as more as if I was connected to an information 'chip' only, rather than close to another being.

My first impression was of a vast land where the heat was stifling and as far as I could see there was no building to attract the eye. There were patches of dense woodland outnumbered in size it would appear by the everlasting sea of tall grasses that stretched as far as the eye could see.

I was hovering a few hundred feet above such a sea of tall grasses, straw coloured, unmoving in what appeared to be the heat of the midday sun. Farther afield, trees framed part of this savanna on three of its sides. Dense, dark and seemingly impenetrable. This had to be the jungle.

The whole scene was one of heat creating an enforced ambience of calm, stillness, and peace. But this belied its true nature. This was nature in the raw, full of passion, hidden depths, teeming with a life of brilliance, exotic colours, birds, animals, insects, flowers, people, all of indescribable beauty mirroring the Creator's cosmic imagination.

Although I had no body to feel the heat, I was aware all around me of the heaviness that heat creates and I too hovered about very slowly in keeping with Nature.

I scanned the area, looking for hints; signs of the life and colour I had only read about or seen on television in this amazing country but everything appeared dormant. No doubt the animals would be lying still or asleep in any accommodating shade they could find and as the song says, any human would be mad indeed to be venturing out in the noonday sun.

I wondered idly what I would be required to do, for something told me this was not a sight seeing trip. I moved slowly along, triggered purely by intent it would seem, for many miles but everywhere was the same. Still, hot, waiting. After some time, I returned back to my original position, the place in which I had first become aware of this vast continent.

I was beginning to think that this was simply yet another spiritual experience after all, when something below me moved. I went down lower. Yes, the long grasses, about five to six feet in height were swaying in small patches creating a rippling effect before parting, as the bodies they hid began to move forward.

Marjorie Sutton

I could see clearly now as the grasses parted to reveal firstly, the tops of hard headwear and men in camouflage uniform. Soldiers. Correction, guerillas. These were guerillas. Lots of them. First one and then another would rise above the grass, peer ahead, and then wave an arm to signal to those behind to move forward. Instinctively I rose higher, wanting to disassociate myself from those hell bent on wreaking havoc in the shocking senseless way that only man can.

I looked down again and saw more movement. Stealthily, silently, grasses moved as if by a gentle whispering wind. I went lower to see what nationality they were but apart from being black I could not tell, could not see their faces clearly, did not want to get too close to those with evil on their mind.

But they were the reason for my being here and I knew that I would have to continue now in what would be a search for their intended victims. As I wondered which direction to take it suddenly occurred to me that they might be superstitious and if I could attract their attention in some way, that in itself might send them running in the opposite direction. I wondered just what I could do, having no form. I knew that if they looked up they would see a round grey blob floating along above them. I don't know how I knew, I just knew, so I tried looping around, up and down, willing just one or two of them to see me and sound the alarm but not one of them looked my way.

I was just wasting time. I had to move on and quickly in the direction they were going obviously but what I was expecting to find I had no idea. It certainly wasn't a single storey building set in a clearing, very ordinary, very civilian, very establishment with a small e.

However this is where I arrived, unannounced, unseen and to all intents and purposes unrequired. As I wandered through the rooms there was no sense of foreboding or alarm. Just people going about their daily routines. I wondered what they were doing in the middle of the Congo.

Quite a large building, it could clearly house a number of people, a few of them children. The people I saw were all white. From its clinical appearance it gave off the feeling of 'station'. Weather station perhaps. It certainly wasn't a military establishment; the vibrations emanating from it were quiet, peaceful and strangely lacking in fear. Whoever was in there did not make up a fighting machine, were probably at this stage unaware of what was stealing towards them.

I was drawn to a large room whose interconnecting walls were made of glass, containing large pieces of machinery, computers perhaps. By today's standard they were enormous and had many dials. It was definitely a communications station, radio or weather I did not know but paper was being spewed out at intervals rather like ticker tape and men were reading them and making notes on charts.

As I looked around the room, I recognised the leader. He was wearing a white shirt and dark trousers, had short dark hair and looked to be about thirty something. I never did see his face but I knew that he was the man in charge, the one I had to direct my efforts to.

This particular room looked into another narrow room, which was at a lower level, again with machines and a couple of men working around them. The leader seemed to keep a watching brief on what was happening below but always he was working hard, concentrating totally on his own work. For a short time I watched as people went about their business. Some rooms quiet, some busy with the happy chatter normally surrounding children. I wondered idly as to their presence here and their education. Perhaps they were visiting their fathers, on holiday. Perhaps there was a village or town close by but this spot seemed to be quite isolated.

I wanted to speak with them, find out who they were, what they knew of the situation outside because I didn't know why any militant group would wish to harm them. It was not to be. No matter how hard I concentrated mentally on contacting one of them, I couldn't get through.

As I looked around me I couldn't see anyone with channels into their energy fields which would have denoted an ability for clairvoyance and as telepathy was all I could use at this time I would just have to keep trying. Even though I had no form, my vibrations or energy fields were still operating and if there had been one with psychic abilities they might have picked up on me and listened to my thoughts, certainly felt my vibrations and thus picked up on me. I was beginning to feel frustrated. Despite lacking the emotional, astral field, this was beginning to get to me.

I did not go outside again over the next two days as I had to use all within my power to make contact. Something else I discovered in this mental state was that time as time had no meaning for me. I only knew that time had passed when darkness descended on me like a blind rolling down and for just a few seconds there was a sense of nothingness.

Then the blind would rise and it was morning again. The darkness didn't envelope me but seemed to be more a black wall in front of me which I had to accept and wait patiently for it to go. I knew by the ongoing activities and the change in light that this blackness did indeed signify a change of day, but I didn't have the time to ponder too much on this extraordinary state as I concentrated hard on trying to make contact.

At times I would go outside and travel back to find out just how much ground the guerillas had made and try to gauge just how much time I had left. For me time went much more quickly than for those inhabiting the physical world and this threw me. What might be deemed a couple of hours in physical time to me, actually constituted a day to them and I was in danger of panicking as I didn't want to be caught out. Working in this way was all brand new to me and I was interpreting events as they happened and trying to make sense out of what I was seeing and doing in what was for me a very strange state of being, albeit clearly a natural one.

Marjorie Sutton

To my surprise the guerillas hadn't made much headway. Perhaps they had had to stop and await further instructions or perhaps they could only make real progress in the cool of the late afternoon and evening. I waited some little time to see in what direction they would move next and when they did continue on line for the station I rapidly went ahead knowing for certain now that I really was on a rescue mission. One that was vitally important and urgent in the extreme.

That evening on my return to the station, instead of going immediately inside I decided to wander around the outer perimeters of the building and look for the normal way from the building to the outside world. In my heart I knew that any way to freedom on foot or by jeep would be covered by the guerillas by the time those in the station became aware of the dangers about them.

I couldn't see signs of a helicopter pad but even if I had, getting the message to these people in the building seemed impossible. Everywhere else seemed to be surrounded by thick jungle, seemingly impenetrable but I knew that there had to be another way, other than the way they would normally use, otherwise why was I there?

I searched for what seemed ages until, to the right of the building, I came across a spot which gave off less dense vibrations. To the naked eye it would be yet more dense jungle but as I went through the outer trees I soon became aware of an old path behind, much overgrown but passable. I lowered myself to the height of a man to see what might be possible.

As I continued along until the trees thinned out down to bushes I knew that this old path would lead them to safety. It would be their only chance.

Going back inside the station I sought out the leader yet again. As always, busy at his work my presence close to him, even when I 'sat' on his shoulder elicited no response. There was no way I could get through to him, no chink in his mental auric field to give him thoughts, hunches, ideas outside that of his work. There was nothing even at the most minimal level that would allow of communication with me. He was bent over his desk, sometimes walking across to the glass wall and the room set slightly below his and he would communicate with the person reading or feeding one of the machines.

I went through the rooms once more, reaching out tentatively into the mental field of each adult. Since my recent absence there had been a profound change. News of disturbances in the area must have filtered through. Eventually my attention concentrated on one man in particular with dark curly hair and a light beard accompanying women and children who were moving around, concern and agitation reflected in their movements.

Just how much they were aware of what was going on outside I did not know, their thought fields being full of their immediate tasks of packing, of gathering together what they could take, of herding the little ones and eventually themselves into one room.

Marjorie Sutton

As I watched I felt their urgency but the urgency for me was how on earth I could get them out of here now that I knew where they must go. Now it would be relatively easy for them. Relief, excitement, exasperation touched me. It was up to me to get them out of here, to effect a rescue but as no one could see or hear me I was beginning to feel frustrated, agitated and dare I say, mental panic wasn't too far away.

I moved from the group to the man in charge but he spent all his time glued to the machines. People were giving him reports from time to time and he was steadfastly occupied in watching one machine. He was totally engrossed in his job, intense, well educated, and well suited no doubt to this insular life, a man of science no doubt.

I tried again, almost attaching myself to his head and yet again tried to speak telepathically with him. I willed with all my might that he pick up on my thoughts but he could neither hear me, feel my presence or pick up the mental graphics I was trying to issue, to show him the trees and the path beyond. I seemed to spend all of one day in this manner, sure that I would in the end break through. There had to be a rest period, a diminution of mental energy being expended when I could perhaps squeeze through just one word, such as ESCAPE and that might lead to other things, allow other thoughts to take shape, to follow on but to no avail. And then, more news seemed to come through one of the machines. The vibrations in the building changed. Fear had taken a hand. Now perhaps I would be able to get through, as their imaginations would begin to work overtime. This it seemed was my only chance. If someone would only begin to think of the possibility of an old path, a possible way through the bush, I was in with a chance.

For the first time I wondered why I wasn't in my astral body. Perhaps then I could have made something move, made a noise, done something. A child perhaps might have been able to communicate with me through their astral bodies at night when they slept for children are particularly good communicators.

Then I knew. Two counts. Firstly, in my astral body I would have become over involved within my emotional field which in turn would have impaired my judgement. I would have got bogged down within the dire circumstances these people found themselves. My efficiency level would have fallen and it was for this reason that I could only make contact with them through telepathy and I didn't need my astral body for that. Secondly, whoever had sent me on this mission must have known that using my mental abilities would be the best chance for me to get through. Had known there was no one there capable of picking up on me in any other way. But they had known too that there was one, just one person who would be willing to follow their hunches and let me in. The rest was down to me.

For the next few days I spent a great deal of time trying to get through to each and every occupant of that building. Nothing. No one would let me in. Until one evening I decided to spend some time on the man with dark curly hair sitting on the floor propped up against an inside wall with little ones around him. They were no longer sleeping in their beds but huddled close together as if for safety.

I knew that time was now running out. I had been once more outside to observe the guerillas, gauge their speed of travel and try to work out just when they would arrive. They were still some two or three miles away and were camped for the night. For some reason they were not pressing on to their final goal. Instead they appeared to be very relaxed, laughing and joking amongst themselves, after all their prey was an easy one, civilian men women and children. They sat around in groups their uniforms unbuttoned, some just in vests. Perhaps they were awaiting the arrival of one who would give the final instructions. And darkly, maybe that, combined with their knowledge that the people in the station had nowhere to go had allowed them to temper their advance.

The man with curly hair, sitting on the floor with his back to the wall looked exhausted but I picked up his thoughts of 'if only there was a way out, he would do anything, *anything.*'

I zoomed in quickly, giving him my thoughts to try just one more time. Look again at the trees at one particular spot. I mentally produced a replica of the area he needed to go to as it was at this time of night at the same time impressing on his mental field the word ESCAPE.

After what seemed forever, to my delight he rose slowly to his feet, spoke to a woman, no doubt to inform her of his mission and went outside. It was of course pitch dark but I was working well now. Giving him the images of strong knives with which to cut through the outer trees I was thrilled to see him walk to an out house and bring out a machete and some other long bladed knife and walk towards the spot behind which the path lay.

I watched as he laboured long and hard. I encouraged him to keep on, giving him the idea of the old path they had all forgotten which might just be there somewhere. After a couple of hours it seemed, he was able to make his way through realising quickly that he really had found an old path. The trees tore at his hair and arms but he could get through. Quickly he ran back inside the station and soon the women and children were filing silently across the clearing and into the jungle, holding hands tightly, following the curly haired man. The relief for me was overwhelming. I went back inside. Just a small number of men remained, still attending machines and charts. Tomorrow hopefully at dawn they would all leave and I could return to my home, mission accomplished.

It was not to be. The leader, when it came to it would not leave his post and I looked on with dismay as he shook his head at the last man to leave. Why was he so insistent on staying. He seemed to think that if and when the fighting men did arrive they would ignore him. Might make life difficult for a time but not enough to make him desert his post. I knew that they would kill him.

I tried again but his auric field was very strong, very resilient to outside forces which can be a good thing, indeed it is a necessary part of our natural defences, but in certain situations a little leeway doesn't come amiss. Being 'open', being willing to listen now and then is a positive necessity. No doubt his excellent scientific mentality had created a barrier to any thing which was not tangible, to his logical mind. If you can't see it, it isn't there. Closed down as he was, I couldn't read his thoughts just as he couldn't read mine.

With a heavy heart I moved in as close as I could and tried yet again to make contact but when someone doesn't have a receptive mind the going is extremely hard. So I settled for hovering behind him, willing him to go. I spoke slowly and repeatedly about the danger but it didn't make the slightest impression. If I could have cried I would probably have sobbed quietly at the futility of it all. He was standing bent over a machine still completely engrossed in what he was doing when they burst in and killed him. Mercifully for me I did not have to watch that awful sight as the blind of darkness rolled down before the final vicious act but I knew that he was dead. I realised with a great sense of sadness and more than a little frustration that I had lost the battle and he had lost his life. It had been an important job or I wouldn't have been given it. Just how important had it been to rescue the one who died? This thought was to occupy my thoughts for years to come.

I returned to the present and this plane with a great sense of loss and failure but I would not allow any feelings of guilt. There is no point in being a martyr to a lost cause. I had been given the challenge and had only partly succeeded but I couldn't have tried harder. Win or lose I had learned that communication with another who was totally blocked from all but the physical was virtually impossible - for me anyhow. But it had taught me a very valuable lesson. Always listen to that still small voice - it may not be yours and it may be a lifesaver!

The concept of Consciousness

In order to accept the possibility of people living, working and 'being' in other dimensions, one has first to recognise just what Consciousness means and how Consciousness manifests. To that end we must do a number of things. We must separate the body from the intelligence within- the Self, Spirit or Soul call it what you will, and understand we are working with two separate and very different forms of intelligence.

The body is a wonderful machine - like intelligence, created by an amazing Creator as a vehicle of experience for another kind of intelligence – the Spirit. Attached to that vehicle and surrounding it completely are a series of energy fields each relating to some aspect the incarnating spirit will need in order to experience life on earth in its chosen form, in this case, that of a human being.

When the spirit takes up residence we call that process Incarnation. Thus, at birth the Indwelling Spirit, Self, or Intelligence Within becomes conscious on the planet Earth ready for its experiential learning programme. That is to say it becomes aware of Itself within this three dimensional vehicle we call the body. Before this moment the Self was conscious elsewhere and is and has always been a 'being' of and in many dimensions. On the Earth it has to experience the experience of being a three dimensional Being- a human being - with all the limitations that implies. But when the Intelligence Within is advanced enough to leave the body and it's earthly limitations, it can and does live or 'be' in a more advanced state of a higher awareness in a higher dimension.

Consciousness is a state of awareness and as the Self becomes aware or conscious in this world, so does the world begin to take shape around it. Thus as a new born baby becomes conscious of its new surroundings and as the body begins to grow and develop very quickly so too does the awareness and the analysis of that awareness or Consciousness. Eventually the individual becomes aware of the physical, the mental and emotional aspects of their being. They begin as toddlers to explore their physical bodies and the feelings which certain acts evoke within the body. Feelings, starting out as perhaps a strange sensation, an unpleasantness or a feeling of well being, trigger off reactions in the physical. Older human beings around- adults - then give these feelings and sensations names and the advancing child accepts the labels.

Marjorie Sutton

Thinking is the most natural aspect of our being but when we try to analyse thoughts, where do they come from, why, and why do some thoughts disappear and some stay and so on, everything becomes very complex. So we don't really give the subject too much attention. We take them for granted for thoughts we have, all the time and 'talking to our Self' we do from birth.

We talk about something called mind. Where is it, what is it? People play mind games, talk about the power of the mind and speak of thoughts being living things. Not many people actually go any further than this. For most, these are just words and they believe they know what is meant by them – a sort of blind, almost abstract understanding.

Mind is not to be found within the physical. Mind is of the spiritual. Mind is ultimately Divine, there being only one. That which created all that there is, used this aspect of Itself to create and just like all creation there are different levels to be found within it, each one providing advancement to something higher, deeper, more spiritual.

That which we call 'my mind' refers to that which can be accessed by us from the Whole, usually only a tiny proportion. As we advance in years and in comprehension and in a desire to know more, then we can advance further into the Whole.

Our brain is a computer like organ programmed to interpret and act upon the thoughts we put into it… It does not know the difference between that which is real or that which is unreal, imaginary, fantasy. It takes on *all* thought processes as if they are real and acts accordingly. This factor is extremely important in understanding that the thoughts are processed as it has been programmed by it's creator so to do. It then passes on the messages you give it to the body and body parts down to the individual cell. In this way it protects the body by initiating the body programme. Thus if we are under attack the brain sets in motion all the preset body preservation data that the body requires to defend itself by initiating the fight or flight program and this takes place in seconds. Such an amazing machine. Such an amazing creator.

It is also a mediator between the spirit within and the overall spirit without. Whilst Mind is not a physical attribute it is accessed to a greater or lesser degree by the indwelling spirit, depending on the maturity of that spirit. The more advanced the spirit the more Mind can be accessed and drawn through to activate the brain. The more we have the ability to tap into different forms of Consciousness the more we are able to access the deeper recesses of Mind and what might be called Collective Consciousness and as we advance further we are able to explore Divine Mind for this too is already a part of us albeit a very small part.

At our present level we are on the fringes, skirting along the outer parameters of Mind, accessing only that which we perceive to be there: simple thoughts which our three dimensional brain can interpret.

Marjorie Sutton

Even the cleverest of people appear to double back on themselves at a particular stage of their development. Instead of going into the outer reaches, forever expanding ideas and the frontiers of knowledge, they backtrack in fear of intolerance and professional exclusion. Wasn't it Martin Luther King who said;

> *"Our scientific power has outrun our spiritual power.*
> *We have guided missiles and misguided men."*

Many remain forever hidebound by what we call scientific fact that very often lesser mortals impose on the masses. Some Men of Science over the centuries have been labelled as heretics by their supposed colleagues simply because they have taken that step further, have dared to reach out and look that little bit further into Mind.

There is that part of Mind which deals purely with the physical form, or should we say that which the physical can respond to, access. It connects closely to the computer like brain and the interpretation of signals via our cells of taste, touch, smell, vision and hearing. Here the interpretation by the brain of the Mind, of what is happening around the body, alerts us to physical dangers. In some part it alerts us to emotional dangers too as we recall past situations similar to the present, this time working within the brains memory banks and mentally we can be alerted to danger just by interpreting a situation mentally…however vaguely…when 'warning bells begin to ring'.

However, we all take these aspects of the human being for granted without paying much attention to the how's, the why's and the wherefore's unless we are trying to analyse others or ourselves, wondering… Just what makes a person tick?

We all are aware of these different aspects or dimensions of our being and spend a great deal of time in one or another of these aspects at various times. For example we are very much in our physical aspect when we concentrate on eating and drinking, making love or fighting. On the other hand we can almost ignore our physical body when the emotional side of us takes over especially in times of fear and grief, not wishing to eat or sleep, as we would normally do.

We are more within our mental fields when we study or need to work something out and we forget or do not want food and drink for long periods of time, especially if we are emotionally involved as well. We can also be aware that we are working within and around all of our aspects all of the time and we take it for granted because we are three dimensional beings.

The physical aspect appears to be all that there truly is, the only tangible part of us that is and yet we know that sometimes our passions rule us but we cannot see this all-powerful aspect of our being. Whilst we recognise an outburst may be due to envy or bitterness, anger or unrequited love, these are only the results of our emotional dimension exerting its influence over us.

Marjorie Sutton

We don't actually see this dimension and because of this we treat it as if it isn't real, as if it isn't there but it is a vital part of our make-up the Self is here to learn about and stabilise in it's quest for more spiritual growth. The *results* of emotional outbursts are there for all to see and we should see the dangers posed if the emotional aspect gets out of control.

Just as the physical aspect needs it's batteries charged, so too does the emotional field and both energy fields are equally important, each having a terrific ripple effect on the other. Great emotional outpourings drain the physical body, create physical problems just as joy and happiness create a sense of well being. We can make ourselves ill through our emotional and mental fields. 'Sick with worry' is a common expression and says it all. We can also make ourselves well but due to man's indoctrination of guilt and fear especially through religion, it is so much easier for the human being to be negative than it is to be positive. Many religions control through fear so children are brought up to be afraid of rather than love the deities involved they are supposed to worship.

The mental aspect or energy field can also become exhausted effecting the nervous system eventually, including the brain. We spend so much time within the mental energy fields, studying, reasoning, talking to ourselves continuously until we can no longer think straight or our mind goes a blank. Yet we don't always see it as we do the physical dimension in terms of importance. Again this is just as real as any physical body.

We use our mental energy field by far the most of any of our energy fields, virtually non stop, and because we cannot see it, take it for granted and don't often give much thought to it. This is our lower mental range and vitally important but not always recognised as such. We don't know what goes on in other people's minds unless they tell us. Without the ability to use telepathy other people's minds are a closed book and yet they all form part of Collective Consciousness or Mind.

On occasions however we realise that we do know what someone is thinking and we are often proved right because at this level it shouldn't be too difficult.

We live eat and breathe amongst three dimensional beings but those of lesser dimensions as we perceive animals and plants to be, we don't even try to communicate with. In our three dimensional world telepathy seems like magic and the possibility of a fourth dimension, pure science fiction for most of the Earth's inhabitants.

We should, if we are the intelligent three dimensional beings we consider ourselves to be, communicate with other life forms we consider to be less intelligent than ourselves but we don't. Instead we miss the opportunity, enclosed in our tiny cocoons of self importance on a planet teeming with life.

The fourth dimension and beyond is still all about awareness, Consciousness, but when we speak of the fourth dimension we are moving into spiritual awareness also, spiritual

Consciousness, that which is beyond the physical third dimension. The laws of physics or perhaps we should say metaphysics still apply and a deeper understanding and access to Mind is mankind's next step but a step not many would think themselves capable of taking.

When we sleep we let go of the physical awareness, moving into the realms of thoughts and emotions as we dream. We call that being Unconscious because we are not fully Conscious in the physical.

The dreams are seen as simply remnants of Consciousness below our physical awareness, our Subconscious. So some form of the word Consciousness itself is brought into play all the time and is a perfectly natural state to be in at whatever level. But people cannot easily project into another Consciousness because it is the unknown, inexperienced state of 'being' for so many. Plus if you are not aware that it is there, you cannot reach it because there is no desire to.

Seeing is believing, is what most people think and the concept of belief allowing you to see is not a popular one. Hence people refuse to accept that which they cannot access with their five senses. If by accident they do, they dismiss it and call it their imagination.

Imagination itself is an immensely powerful tool without which the world would cease to exist. It is the creative part of Mind – ours and the Creator's and must never be dismissed as unimportant or useless. Without it we would cease to exist. Imagination is visual perception, vital for life and on another level, fantasy and all too often fantasy is mistakenly perceived to be a form of lying or fabrication, a negative thing. Whereas fantasy is simply a word that means something made up. How can anyone possibly imagine or fantasise that which does not exist. Each part of the fantasy must relate to something(s) they have seen on this or any other level. What can be quite wrong is the interpretation by the three dimensional brain. But we can't imagine anything we have no concept of on one or other levels of our being.

We know when we are trespassing in another dimension or another realm because we cannot imagine what we have never first seen. Imagination is creating fantasies using the images we are accustomed to. Anything we have never seen before cannot therefore be imagination or fantasy and must be from another dimension.

Most people are locked in a cocoon of present awareness and we are indoctrinated by religious belief systems, scientific 'fact' and a disturbing lack of experience of other dimensions to even look into the concept of other dimensions, other worlds, except of course for the quantum physicists.

Throughout the centuries, we have been told it is not for us to understand because *they* don't, *they* with the power. If they cannot do it, no one can and besides, other worlds are to do with God. You either believe in them or you don't. And if God wanted you to know He would show you. The fact that this information is our natural heritage and a necessary part of our spiritual progression, seems to be overlooked. Their

God is obviously a very secretive God relishing in power, man power. A God made in man's image.

The very possibility of other planets with life in other galaxies should at the very least allow us to explore other dimensional concepts as part of our education as evolving beings. Even evolving human beings.

Being absorbed in the third dimension is very limiting so let us expand our horizons and see just how it is possible to become aware in other dimensions whilst still alive here.

Consciousness IS. A degree of Consciousness is all there is. It isn't born, it doesn't die. Only the physical is born and eventually dies, when the necessary experience the Self requires has been fulfilled and the experiential learning programme has been achieved.

When Consciousness leaves the physical body it is automatically fully conscious of the dimension or plane it finds itself in or on. It immediately expands and blends in with all Consciousness just as a drop of water falling into the ocean becomes part of the ocean.

There is a greater awareness, a greater sense of being, of encompassing all that there is. One immediately knows much more because one is in contact with much more, that which we might call Collective Consciousness.

Whilst at the human level, still incarnating in a physical form from time to time on Earth, we are aware of ourselves as individuals but elsewhere when this life has ended there is also a greater awareness of the group. It is indeed a totally different world and we can do totally different things in it, automatically, because this is not a stepping stone, a learning place, it is our real home. However, viewed from this world, the next step is gigantic and possibly at first unbelievable.

There, a thought immediately triggers off action. For example, the desire to see someone or a particular place is all it takes to be there with them or be in that place. We don't go there, we are in some part of our aspect already there, so travel as we know it on earth ceases to be. But if we take form, the awareness is lessened and time and space become more as we know it to be. So returning to the physical body means that we come out of the ocean and go back to being the bubble with all its limitations, it's smallness in every possible sense. Within this environment we can really only be aware of that which surounds and imprisons us.

The difference between the two states of being is enormous and takes a great deal of getting used to, especially being the bubble as this is not our natural state as spiritual beings.

One has to understand that just as there is no break in the flow between the physical, the emotional or the mental in our every day lives, so too does the flow of life throughout Consciousness continue elsewhere all the time.

A life we cannot normally see because the vibrations are different, makes form as we know it invisible but nevertheless there is form and it is just as real in its own dimension as ours is in this. Life goes on in many, many dimensions without halt. Our not being aware of those in other dimensions doesn't mean they don't exist.

It is like being in a locked room without doors or windows. Never having known anything else, anything else does not exist. We become submerged literally in a small confining space.

When people for a number of reasons do exist outside their bodies it is the essential Self without physical form, a natural phenomenon, not a frightening concept. If they simply leave the physical body and stay put, very much attached to their physical Consciousness they will see their physical surroundings albeit with somewhat different aspects.

A near death experience is quite simply that. If the body is not safe the Self will leave if the shock to the system is big enough and return when it recognises that the body can still sustain life. Some people experience this. Others who have a similar experience, on finding themselves still conscious but outside of their physical body may immediately think they have died. Beginning to think about that aspect will bring about a sensation of floating towards something, usually a light or a person who has passed on who may give them a gentle nudge back towards their body. It can be a very beautiful experience that they will always remember and they will never be afraid of 'dying' again.

We must now also take a closer look at the energy systems, which go to make up our present existence. It would appear that there are seven, one each to stimulate and provide energy for each of the seven different aspects of our being. They are, the etheric, the emotional or astral, the three levels of mental and the spiritual.

The etheric supports the physical body - matter. It is the 'vitality' field permeating every cell of the physical identically. So we have an identical etheric Liver, Heart, Skin etc. It is the vitality field of the body. When the physical body dies and begins to decompose it is thought that so too does the etheric disintegrate, there being no further need for it.

On Earth this is true but there is a different role for the etheric structure farther afield within the etheric itself. I am referring now to the wider etheric around the planet and indeed between planets in outer space. But the etheric does leave the physical body at death. Phycisists working in this field have discovered that a new corpse emits a charge for many hours after death.

The amount of time it takes for this, the etheric energy field to leave depends on the manner of dying. A natural death where the body is preparing to die, winding down, taking less and less energy on board, depleting naturally should discharge the remaining energy in two or three days.

A sudden death will take longer as there is more energy to release and to self destruct in the prime of life can take longer still. People commit suicide for many reasons so some are full of energy and others are deeply depleted at that time so the amount of energy to be discharged will differ.

We must not however confuse the energy field and the departing Spirit. The etheric field still charging is not an indicator that the spirit is still there.

When we finish our time here and we need to return from whence we came, we still need our emotional (astral), mental and spiritual energies in order to work in those dimensions and planes of existence. It is the same if we are only leaving the body for a small period of time. Self departs surrounded by those energy fields it will need whilst it is away, whilst retaining the connections necessary to keep life flowing within the physical form. This connection is spoken of as the silver cord but is in fact a vibration not a solid piece of matter.

The silver cord appears to be attached to the Solar Plexus which is our connection to the realms of spiritual awareness, other dimensions, other worlds. It is down this vibrational structure that the message is sent from the physical intelligence when it is necessary for the travelling Spirit to return. Likewise the feeling of a 'presence' from another dimension is first felt at the solar plexus because messages can travel two ways. First we 'know' and then our thoughts assail the mental organ, the brain, almost instantaneously and then we can hear or see by using telepathy.

The emotional, the mental and spiritual energy fields will surround the travelling spirit in order for that spirit to access the particular planes or dimensions one is visiting.

When we are psychically aware, our Consciousness inhabits another dimension the emotional or astral as it is often referred to, where we then have to use the astral tools in order to make sense of what is around us. Here we pick up on another's emotional state and see beyond the physical, beyond the smiling face to the torment which lies behind it or recognise the evil beyond the charm and can pick up on people's thoughts to a greater or lesser degree even unto telepathy and we become 'knowers'.

Being a knower doesn't mean that one knows everything all the time but at certain times and in certain situations the knowers are never wrong even when they have only just met someone or are simply given information about a situation. It is an automatic opening of a door which allows us to see very clearly.

Clairvoyants and mediums use these facilities. It is a natural ability and many people have psychic ability to one degree or another. Depending on belief systems usually, it can either be openly acknowledged, turned into superstition or pushed firmly to one side in ignorance and fear.

We have all experienced psychic ability in our lives and we can develop that sixth sense if we choose but again religious belief systems may prohibit this. We should all use our hunches, our gut feelings, our natural abilities, as much as possible. A great deal of heartache could be saved if we did.

When we don't use these facilities we are turning our back on our own safety systems, our own higher self, that in itself is a perverted way of looking at the incredible systems the Creator gave us in order to live life on Earth to the full.

Marjorie Sutton

During an astral projection or 'out of body', the physical body is perfectly safe as long as the Spiritual connection to it remains. If the body is disturbed, a vibration sets up immediately in the other energy fields and the intelligence within returns to its body in an instant. We cannot measure the time but when one is out of body, working, there is always the knowledge that there is only so much time from the point of view of the physical aspect before we must return.

If one has to return quickly for any reason we usually know as we feel as if we have just thudded down at great speed into the body. It seems to be the three dimensional brain's interpretation of events and we can even feel winded, the thud is so great.

The concept of Consciousness can be seen and understood clearly when we accept the reality of a three dimensional existence whilst looking at the awareness of one and two-dimensional concepts of certain life forms. Particular beings who do not have a three dimensional aspect cannot conceive of more than the flat square, the circle, having no concept of width and depth. We as three-dimensional beings understand the concepts of width and depth and therefore can understand the measure say, of a cube opposed to a square or a sphere opposed to a circle.

Up to three dimensional we all exist on the same planet but our awareness and understanding of the world we all live in is quite different depending on which of the energy fields we inhabit the most.

It is said that when Darwen arrived at the Galapagos Islands, the natives wondered how he could possibly have sailed such a distance in such a small boat. Explaining that they had only travelled to shore in the rowing boat but that the ship out at sea had carried them there, they didn't understand. They couldn't see the ship because they were not aware that such a large vessel could float - therefore it didn't exist and wasn't seen by the natives.

Hence we must open our minds to the possibilities in order to 'see' what is actually there. When we can do this we can begin to understand other dimensions.

Quantum physicists can produce formulae and mathematical structures to explain other dimensions and parallel worlds but until we accept those possibilities as a race, accept our heritage for ourselves openly, we are unable to go forward as a race and experience the reality for ourselves.

The Power of Thought

Thoughts are living things and with our thoughts we create, eventually, reality in physical terms. We create our homes, our communication systems, our environment, our relationships and our problems, all by the amazing power of thought. The more we concentrate on a thought, the more we make it more real, more solid within our own energy fields and within the energy fields of the plane we are conscious in, which in turn will affect us for good or bad.

We can bring things into physical being by the power of thought. Without it nothing would exist. We spend all our days thinking, creating powerful images that remain around us within the energy fields: hence the notion of only thinking positive thoughts if we want to have a positive life.

Negative thoughts have the reverse effect and so many people fulfil their own negative prophecies because they cannot let go of fear or jealousy or hate and bitterness; surrounding themselves with negative images that are becoming more concrete, more real, every day.

We can send thoughts to another, for good or bad, unwittingly or deliberately so that across these dimensions and within these dimensions there can be real blockages occurring as thought forms become stronger and more fixed within that particular dimension.

The man of science with a particular project or invention in mind will have it occupy all his thoughts until it is a tangible part of his being, completely attached to him. This is good because he can add to or detract from at will in his mind until he comes up with the answer.

The auric field, our energy system is like a storage house or a workshop into which we can dip at leisure, returning yet again to perfect that which we seek to create. It is the same with great composers or artists. Theirs is a way of life where their particular subject is the centre of their universe. Having a good idea will get you nowhere unless and until you make it real in this and other dimensions. But once the ideal has been achieved, the creation now complete in the physical world, the mental prototype can be dissolved.

Around the earth in these other dimensions there is a great deal of clutter which needs to be disposed of in order for the power and the currents to run smoothly for the planet and all its inhabitants. Ideas which are not concentrated on, eventually dissipate but as long as you return to them you will keep them in situ.

Marjorie Sutton

We can create almost concrete life forms around the planet as well as around ourselves and this effects people's own energy fields. There is a big ripple effect from one to another and back again.

Many people suffer illness because of the memories of tragic events occurring in their childhood because their thoughts of that time are still there within their energy fields. The emotional energy field is often full to bursting with old thought forms. Something which happened fifty years before, is still affecting people at the 'very thought' of it is just as real as that which happened yesterday and can have an extremely detrimental effect on the physical body.

It is a good idea for all of us to remove clutter from our own energy fields by becoming aware of the damage we do to ourselves and others we are close to, by holding on to the past in a way which is not helpful.

We can learn from the past by the experience, not by keeping old grudges alive. We harm ourselves too by harbouring quite literally, keeping and protecting silly thoughts, within our fields. Pretending that this or that is going to happen or could happen, usually based on fear.

Energy transmits thought waves at a terrific pace and one person's fear can affect large numbers almost simultaneously as the connections are brought into play. But this can happen for good too and if we could all do a global healing meditation every day, we would soon be inhabiting a wonderful new planet.

So thoughts and the concept of thought should play a conscious role in our everyday lives, understanding that as we think, so we are.

It is important to recognise our personal responsibility for our thoughts and the damage they may do to another. Everyone has connections to other dimensions and thoughts travelling around can be picked up by anyone, especially the unstable, the young and the elderly who are frail as they just get 'bad thoughts' and cannot deal with them as fit, mature people might.

This applies to all those people with addictions who daily damage their own protective shields allowing mischief and sometimes worse in.

Energy fields around the person and the planet originally have a protective sheath which can be damaged by trauma to the person or the planet. Negative thought forms can enter energy fields forming a negative magnet which will attract negative energies.

Healing through the energy fields will repair the protective shields once the negative energies have been dispelled and bad thoughts can be dissipated. Many forms of anxiety and mental illness are caused by such damage to the protective shield. Drugs unfortunately can sometimes add to the damage as they seek to address by suppression only, physical symptoms.

Anything which is only suppressed instead of dealt with can only have a detrimental effect. The misuse of drugs as found in those with addictions also damages this protective sheath.

Marjorie Sutton

When someone has an out of body, the consciousness leaves the physical and becomes aware of the other dimensions around the planet. It can also be immediately aware of that which is cluttering up that particular dimension in a particular area and what is seen can appear to be very frightening until one realises that what is there is not an intelligence in itself.

It is simply the prototype and one can, by bringing energy to bear upon it, clear it away. If particular thought forms around a house or a war zone are so solid as to appear real we have to realise that we are able to destroy the thought forms around us.

But if people creating those thought forms do not change they will simply create more and reinforce them hourly or daily. To get rid absolutely we have to stop people from thinking the thoughts in the first place and we have to do this on the physical level through a change of attitude.

We have to educate people to make them aware of the power of the mind, the power of thought. We need not worry that those with evil on their mind will use it too. They already do. They are adepts.

We have to make the rest of mankind aware of their potential to override on the simple premise that light will always dispel darkness. We can also help to clear the clutter by doing a global healing meditation and if necessary, a personal healing meditation.

Psychic Attack

The words Psychic Attack often conjures up images of so called other worldly entities having a go at people either by appearing to and frightening them or strange, ghoulish beings attaching themselves to their body or their home. I am not aware that either of these notions are correct.

The words themselves conjure up a fear and a belief that the attack will take place and is completely out of control of any individual. This is not necessarily so. Whilst psychic attack is not pleasant it is carried out by people in this world through the power of their mind and it is only as strong as their intentions are.

Many people harbour hatred, anger, jealousy and bitterness for years and the person they harm the most is themselves. The feelings and the thoughts are manufactured within and so within is where the harm is done. Poisons are set up within their own bodies that can destroy them.

Marjorie Sutton

It is true that thoughts are living things but that doesn't mean 'entities' - those amorphous blobs from who knows where. Thoughts are alive in the sense that they are creative. Nothing is or can be created unless it is first thought of and by acting on those thoughts we create the reality.

Hence an architect will first think, then put his ideas on paper, then enlarge the ideas into drawings and when the final picture is produced, another will come along and build it, thus making it happen. The more effort he puts into his ideas - his thoughts - the more complete and 'solid' they will become. Physically however, they have to take shape in matter to become reality, solid and obvious.

Our own everyday thoughts conjure up images or fantasies sometimes fleeting and quickly forgotten or concentrated, enlarged, dwelled upon until they are constantly filling our minds.

As we dwell on them, they begin to take on a life of their own and herein lies the dangers. The mind is the most powerful tool we have and because mind waves are strong, the more energy we give them, the more 'real' they become.

Each image dwelt upon consistently and constantly takes on an energy of its own and even when we begin to let go of the obsessional thought, the image will remain strong for years in some cases and will remain within the energy systems of the person who manufactured them.

Just as our memories of real events are stored within our memory banks, so too are our emotional creations kept within our energy systems unless we deliberately and consciously destroy them.

In this way we are all probably guilty of creating psychic attacks upon ourselves without ever considering such a thing might be possible.

Very often these often blurred images come to the fore to the individual who believes they are seeing clairvoyantly, beings from another dimension, another world but they are only seeing their own self made images which flash on the inner eye. These are usually colourless, grey, dark forms which are often flitting to the surface.

Beings from another plane do not have the time or the inclination to potter on this level. These darker images can be annoying, frightening even but because they seem to be so real they are mistakenly thought of as demons or simply those with mischief on their mind.

The owner of these life forms can destroy them and should do as quickly as possible. They clutter up the energy systems and create blockages which in turn can have a real effect on the well being of the physical body eventually.

If we look at the damage done to us via trauma or abuse as children, we see not only the recurring flashbacks from our memory banks but also the feelings which assail us from time to time. These feelings which don't appear to relate to anything in particular often present as strange, sometimes unnerving and unpleasant feelings. These feelings with good analysis skills will often unfold as the thoughts and feelings we had when going through a dreadful time. It is only by that recognition, by accepting, acknowledging and then dealing with them can we finally get rid of them out of our emotional and mental energy fields.

Destroying old thoughts and images can be done in a very positive, creative way. It doesn't have to be a negative project. Indeed it must be done in such a way as to repair the particular energy system in question and not simply leave what might be called scar tissue through which energy cannot flow. Although getting rid of negative static images is a step in the right direction it is only a step and much further work has to be done for a full repair to take place.

Many visualisation techniques used for positivity will eventually work if the imagery is constantly repeated, the more you can 'see' the image the more real it becomes, not in a solid physical way but in an energy way and this has a ripple effect on the body when done properly.

Positive energy creates its own whirlpool attracting more positive energy which can only have a good effect on the overall energy systems of the body which in turn affects the physical well being of the person.

Psychic attack is a step up from verbal attack. Just as sound waves can create havoc at a certain vibrational intensity so too can mind waves affect the physical at a given intense vibrational impact. Both sound waves and mind waves travel over large areas both around the earth and out into space until they are absorbed into the collective wave. But the people who send out harmful waves are usually much closer to home.

One should understand that psychic attack being undertaken by someone who is vaguely miffed by an event will not produce harm in the other person. Most of the time people are not aware of the power of their minds and their abilities to affect another from a distance, non physically and the thoughts are left to dissipate, leaving their owner with a headache or a depression.

But a person who is obsessed with jealousy or the fear of losing someone, something attributable to a particular individual can cause real harm. If the concentration and the continuation of the thought fills their mind day and night and there is a real harmful intention to another, then that other will be affected.

Not only do people think the thought they also talk ceaselessly to themselves about that person, what they would like to see happen to them - pictorially- which can go on with great ferocity for days and weeks or even months because they just cannot leave it alone.

When this happens the thoughts are sent to the hated person as strongly as if they were contacted by telephone and they build up day by day in that persons immediate vicinity. Then, when the person is feeling exhausted and crashed out, their energy guard is not as strong and the bad thought energies can enter not only the energy systems of that person but also the physical body via the nervous system.

The result of this is often a setting up of depression and even panic situations, edginess and a strange fearfulness may begin to overcome them eventually causing them to seek medication or to give them a loss of awareness causing accidents. Once this situation sets up, other negative thoughts being sent gain access easily.

The saddest thing about all this is that even the nicest, kindest, loveliest person can be responsible for psychic attack without knowing it. We are all capable of it and the thoughts lingering around any given street or town in this world will be of a negative nature some of the time.

Everyone has disappointments, broken love affairs, bereavements that all bring about bad thoughts about another or a group of people and all too often the thoughts get out of hand. Most people if they understood the harm that is done in this way would not on reflection wish to harm another or indeed be harmed in such an intrusive and powerful way.

There are however those who know the power of the mind and it is truly their intention to harm as much as possible. In certain cultures this can further degenerate into voodoo. There is nothing wrong with energy or mind just the way we use them.

Being assailed constantly by negative thoughts can bring about both acute and chronic illness. Being a strong, sceptical person who simply doesn't accept such things putting it down to silly superstition will not save you from such an assault, as I know to my cost.

I was made aware of all matters connected with psychic attack one night. I had not been asleep long when I was awakened in my bedroom but within my astral body. I was aware of two doors leading into my bedroom whereas in reality there was only one. This I noticed first.

A voice was saying to me. 'Watch and listen.' Immediately through the extra door opposite my headboard came a moving tower of compacted thoughts; scenes and figures compressed into crumpled box like containers much as one would find in a car dump after the cars had been through the crusher. Grey, moving quickly and the squeak of voices coming from it rather like an audiotape that is played too fast.

As soon as I saw this I shifted back into my physical body just in time to feel the passage of this horrendous tide entering my nervous column and going straight into my body. The feeling was truly awful.

'Why did you let that happen, when you knew?' I cried to my spiritual mentor.

'Because you didn't believe that you could be affected. You didn't believe that because you were not afraid of anyone or anything that you therefore couldn't be harmed and now you know you can. You had to learn the hard way - as usual. We will transfer energies now and get rid of them for you but you must understand that this is around you ALL the time and from now on it is up to you to protect yourself. Personal responsibility!'

Marjorie Sutton

I leaned back on my pillows, exhausted, thanked them for their love and asked how best to protect myself in the present situation, images already forming in my mind as to who was responsible. I was assured that the images were correct but the main problem was how to be protected. I was instructed to spend half an hour a day before going to sleep bringing the white light - itself an intention of positive energy- through and into my auric fields filling them with light over and over again.

When I had finished, I was to seal myself inside my energy cocoon with love. The seal was a one way system, I could give but not receive unless I chose to open up. I was to think of the person(s) responsible for these thoughts with compassion and send the message out mentally to them, to stop. Any further thoughts of this nature would be returned to them. As soon as they hit my shield they would be instructed to be returned to sender. I was also to image the senders in a cocoon of white light to help them with their own problems and keep myself and others safe from them.

I pondered on the meaning of the second door in my bedroom and then realised that this was the way in for these thoughts. What I could see I could guard against but psychic attack often comes from those you never think about; people who often have very little to do with you directly. These people are jealous of the people or objects around you or perhaps just by being who and what you are, can trigger dark emotions in another.

So it doesn't come amiss to recognise if you have however unwittingly hurt someone, or just by being there you are the focus of another's negative thoughts, guard yourself in this way. And if you have such negative thoughts, understand the harm that they do and zap them as they occur. It isn't easy to think nice things all the time. Life isn't fair. People do cheat. You may be a victim of injustice but please do not go down the road of obsessional thinking.

In the end, whilst harm may be done to another, the biggest harm will always be done to yourself. If you create a factory of explosives and poisons within your system, you will eventually self-destruct.

If you believe you may have images within your emotional and mental energy systems which are best removed, then begin now to tackle the problem. Try to find a suitable friend who will take the time to work with you. If this is not appropriate, seek out a counsellor or therapist as the images you wish to remove may need to be analysed first.

The image should be seen to melt away until it is gossamer thin when it will float away. If you have difficulties at this stage, worrying about it, every time the old image appears, replace it with a beautiful thought. Perhaps a scene from a holiday or a beautiful flower or a favourite person and always see energy flowing around you in concentric circles denoting movement.

See different colours because colours are simply different vibrations of energy and make sure that the colours are never static but free flowing and do this until you become a rainbow of colour. As the image begins to fade, speak to it gently from your heart, everything must be done with love and explain why it has to go and or be replaced by another more ideal, positive image.

If you can work so hard that you end up with an aura without static images so much the better. Nothing should be stored up but once enjoyed should be allowed to float away which would then keep blockages to a minimum and easily dispersed.

It is the same on our journey in this realm, we should always keep moving. It is not spiritually healthy to spend too long in the valley or on the highest peak but instead we should take and make the most of what our particular path shows us.

Looking down on the valley and up to the mountain, beauty can be found everywhere and our path will always lead between the two if we do but recognize everything along the way but it must always be our earnest endeavor to reach the end of the path, our one true goal. Sometimes we take many paths as our destiny dictates but we must always remember there are no short cuts and that all our experiences are valuable if they teach us an understanding of ourselves or another, thus allowing us to grow spiritually.

This And Other Dimensions

When we speak of dimensions, we are simply looking at an extra aspect to a person, an object, a situation or a concept; a measure perhaps of their worth rather like an extended unseen boundary. The word itself suggests the awareness of there being more than meets the eye. Sometimes we see the different dimensions or aspects of people through their personal qualities or a new found understanding of a situation will be perceived until a whole new dimension opens up, a whole new way of looking at things. So there is always more to everybody and everything than there might appear to be and once we begin to go down that road we begin to realise that there is always more and more and more.

All living beings have these other dimensions surrounding or in addition to that which we can experience through our five senses. We are all conversant with charm, ambience, attraction, repulsion, good or bad vibes. These are all dimensions of an individual or a place. That certain 'something' that precipitates a mutual understanding of a person or a place that cannot always be put into words. It's a 'feeling' thing that cannot be expressed by words, that intangible something that is a part of our everyday lives from birth to death. Yet, we take it no further in the sense that whilst we bring it into our physical awareness, an integral part of our existence, so far and no further seems to be the unwritten law.

Thus when we turn our attention to 'other dimensions' we are referring to a similar but more subtle understanding of the space or dimension around us. And not just around us but also the around the planet itself.

There are many people in the world who, down the ages, have become aware of these other dimension and the communications that we can make with others on different planes. We call these people psychics, mediums, knowers. And down the years much has been revealed to mankind through the mediumship of communication through the dimensions surrounding us; those bridges and corridors that link the other planes of existence around but outside of the physical dimension.

In order to better understand what going 'out of body' or 'astral traveling' means we need to start in the physical and move outwards.

The dimensions we all take for granted relate to the physical, the emotional, the mental and the spiritual aspects surrounding us, on a very close, personal level. This is because our physical life involves to one degree or another all these aspects that are a part of our essential make up as human beings.

The Physical Dimension

We all touch the physical world with our physical bodies which includes seeing with the physical eyes that which is of a physical nature and so on with all our five senses. These are our physical tools. Here, only the physical is clear, plain, obvious. We all see and hear, touch, smell and taste in exactly the same way unless one or more of these faculties are impaired. We hear of the blind operating more sensitively, using their sixth sense, becoming more aware of their surroundings, of the characters of people and so on, almost as if they are existing in some way, perhaps half way into another dimension.

Those who can pick up on another's vibrations or the different energies in a room are known as 'sensitives' and all but the most insensitive can tell immediately when people have been arguing recently in that room or read and feel other emotions in the air. But most people do not look for anything more, do not seek to learn about just how far this type of communication spreads.

Around each life form and the planet itself these dimensions exist and they do so in a very real way. They are not figments of our imagination. We enter one or the other of them through a 'conscious' process. We need to take it a step further and recognise the *reality* of these other dimensions in as much as we can enter them and those on other planes of existence can also enter them. Dimensions are the connecting pathways between here and there. *Real corridors of Power* where people of like mind can, often in the sleep state venture forth and make real contact with others who likewise are out of body or are from another dimension.

Healers sometimes operate on this level. Many clients over the years have rung to thank me for helping them the previous night. They haven't seen me but they have felt my presence, heard my voice telepathically, just known I was by their side. It has never fazed any of them and they speak as if it is the most natural thing in the world. Which it is.

It can be a meeting place between two worlds or planes of existence. It is important to recognize that this is not a place in which one lives but a place that one may visit and then return back to the plane from which they came.

The Astral Dimension

When we travel out of body in the astral form, in the astral dimension, the form appears to be the same but the tools we use there are quite different. No doubt it is the molecular structure that is different, that enables us to vibrate on a different level, allowing us to exist perhaps in a much faster moving space. From this astral dimension we can see the physical world clearly. It is after all but a step away. But people in the physical dimension for the most part do not see beyond the physical with their physical eyes because the vibrations do not allow.

In the astral dimension we only have to think of someone or someplace and we are almost immediately there. Sometimes when we are there, people in the physical dimension do sense us and their interpretation of what they are sensing is determined by superstition, ignorance, horror films and the like unless they too understand what is happening. Sadly the unknown, unseen, usually precipitates fear where non is needed. For the majority of people, their knowledge of and therefore sense of the astral dimension is a blank.

To work within the astral dimension and see/hear for oneself just what is happening along those busy corridors is truly amazing. Many people leave their body when asleep but they never venture further than the immediate vicinity, returning swiftly as they awake. To spend time in that dimension gives us a greater awareness if needed that one is indeed a spiritual being first and foremost and that life does indeed go on without the encumbrance of the physical.

From the astral dimension we can watch people living on the physical plane, sense their distress. We can walk through the physical walls or matter as our molecular makeup is so different just as it is in water or wood or gas. We can travel around the world literally at will or sit next to someone on a bus without anyone knowing. To all intents and purposes it is very similar to being in the physical in the way we act and react to situations, always aware of ourselves as having form just as we do on Earth but without the restrictions we have to endure in form on Earth.

When one leaves the physical in order to work in one's own astral body (field of energy) whilst still around the third dimension, around the earth, the same joy found on other planes is not there. Everything appears drab, grey, black and white although one knows what colours are being reflected. There is a weightier feel to the Self and one can feel the emotions of others still in the physical as if from a distance so that whilst it has no noticeable effect on the observer one knows the amount of feeling the physical body is experiencing. In this way one is affected by things which are happening in the physical even though a dimension is separating them.

It is a silent world in one sense as one hears differently. There is not the same noise although one is aware because one has experienced it, when noise occurs. One sees and knows. For example, if a volcano erupts one is aware of the deafening roar without experiencing it directly for oneself and thus it does not impale on the senses in quite the same way.

The sense of touch cannot be the same as the different vibration means that the physical matter is not available to us but again we know because of experience what other people are feeling when we see them hurt by a car or touch something hot. However we are simply observers.

We can look through pages of a book instead of having to flip them over which saves a great deal of time. We do not smell although we can sense when something is wrong and what that something is. We know that true roses smell beautifully but the faculty of smell is not there. It is all very much like watching a video, watching life on Earth, except that we can get right in there with the players.

Life forms exist in their astral, mental or spiritual aspect which means that whilst the spirit exists there, it may not always have form; it may simply 'be'. But these corridors of the spirit are free flowing and sometimes overflowing, especially in times of war and great calamity where there are large ongoing movements from Earth. Our connections to these other areas are perfectly normal and natural but like everything else we know so very little about, there are always those who will seek to access inappropriately.

If we go there to help in some way and this event happens very naturally, then there will not be a problem; our energy make up is such that we are advanced enough to do this. But if we try to manipulate our energy systems in order to experience an out of body, then there can be dire consequences. It should be a natural event which means that one's energy fields and one's spiritual makeup has the knowledge and the dynamics to withstand other outside forces. When this is not so, people can be damaged for life via the nervous systems and end up complete nervous wrecks, not to mention the fear they surround themselves with forever after.

When one is out of body occupying one's own astral or mental energy fields or bodies, ones is operating within the corresponding energy fields around the planet. One does not go into another person's energy fields. *Another cannot enter your physical body*. We all have our cosmic fingerprint and as long as we live, another being just would not fit. Apart from anything else there is no point. One can do everything far better through the mental and emotional fields. The physical body is very slow and cumbersome in comparison. They can however come close. One can communicate through telepathy or give love and healing to the physical body. One cannot do more than that. The person who is fully conscious within the physical body may feel someone close to them. One may have a sudden awareness of a presence that may be so strong that they know who it is and can pick up the message before the sensation fades away. Again, sensitives and mediums too can do this as they have developed their psychic abilities.

Anyone can be aware of a loved one close just by suddenly thinking of them in the middle of doing something before all too soon, the moment has gone.

This can also happen without another being out of body. Strong thoughts will reach the person in much the same way and people with a very strong bond will latch on immediately their 'other half' sends thoughts out to them be it a partner or a twin. Soul mates, twins and other closely bonded people always know from a distance, when help is needed.

In a way, other dimensions may be seen as the hidden side of things but these dimensions occupy real space and are where we create and recreate our worlds through our emotions and thoughts. People, spirit, on Earth do not live in these dimensions so much as visit them and use them whilst inhabiting the physical body the majority of the time. Those living on other *planes* can come close to us through these dimensions in order to connect to the earth plane and thus through these connections, to the individual energy fields where they can make their presence known to the individual still in a physical body. We can both visit each other by meeting within these dimensions, a sort of half way house and this does sometime happen when a loved one has passed and people talk about very strong dreams which weren't dreams, where they meet up again.

So, from these other dimensions, when we are out of body we can see the earth and it's inhabitants going about their daily business. We can sense whether they are doing good or doing evil, whether they are happy or unhappy and we can try to influence them through the power of the mind but that is all. We have no power over them BUT if they are open to suggestion, we can work in that way which means, *as like attracts like,* that we can help or hinder them if they have the ability to pick up on us. We can put positive thoughts into their head or negative ones which brings us full circle. We are as we think. We create what we are. We must protect ourselves at all times. When dreadful thoughts come into our head we should be aware that danger lurks and immediately get rid of them.

Everyone is protected to a certain degree so it isn't easy to get through to a person in another dimension or even from another dimension to this one by thought. The problems arise when the persons protective shield is damaged perhaps through trauma or drugs and then the door is open to other energies, other influences which, if the individual is a weak character, having little to do or think about, the thoughts have ready access. These thoughts can be of the mischievous kind and is reminiscent of the old adage, 'the devil finds work for idle hands'.

There are many variables of the experience depending on the person trying to communicate and the person on this level being open, literally to their influence. The strong person here will be safe and still be a good communicator and receiver but only because they *choose* to do this work, as the very good mediums do. Here there is a deliberate opening up of the protective shield to allow communication and they close the door very firmly once the communication is over.

The communicator in another dimension may be working out of body and still living here or they may be visiting from another plane and these will be strong characters for good or bad. People always assume that evolved beings must be good but as we know to our cost, people can be evolved and use their knowledge and skills for ill intent. Like really does attract like. It is the easiest and quickest way to make contact.

If one is a child of the Light then the Light will be all around. The intention is all. If you seek only to do no harm and try very hard to do good then you are automatically a child of the Light and as Light dispels darkness, there is nothing to be afraid of. The biggest problem is ignorance creating fear, creating superstition, creating more fear. As fear is self perpetuating, it can, if left to run its course, destroy. In reality, there is nothing to be afraid of, nothing one cannot handle – except fear itself. Remember that all the darkness in the world, this and others, cannot put out the light from one small candle.

The Spiritual Dimension

The Spiritual dimension is always around everything that lives, here, there and everywhere in the cosmos. It is intelligence unconfined, connected to all other intelligences. The collective consciousness just IS. We are at liberty to tap into this almighty sea of knowledge and experience whenever we wish and we do this most when in true meditation. The individual only uses that which they are able to access but it is there for all of us all of the time. Meditation should teach us how to expand our consciousness, our awareness of all matters we seek to understand, in order to grow and develop spiritually. This in turn impacts on the individual and the group soul and when these have learned and experienced sufficiently they will be able to move and live and have their being in a higher dimension. I.E. from the third into the fourth dimension. So there are no corridors or bridges to that we can call the spiritual dimension as we are connected constantly wherever we are to all Spirit. Mind is collective consciousness and divine mind that which eternally creates more and more and more for us to access.

These and Other Planes

Planes are where people live and work in total consciousness for a period of time just as we do on Earth. The biggest difference is that one may live on a plane for differing periods of time depending on the need of the individual or group. There may be short periods or the period may last for hundreds of earthly years. The planes noted here are those connected to and influencing the planet Earth only.

The Earth Plane

When the time and the need is appropriate, the soul will continue to re incarnate again on Earth to further his learning and his advancement spiritually. The whole point of life on earth seems to be that of experiencing the experience, of learning to work through personal choice within a big emotional dimension which can be almost always a destabilising factor in all our decisions. As evolving Spirit we need to learn to stabilise this side of us so that the whole of us becomes stable – safe and sound so that in other dimensions and other worlds we will be developed enough to make decisions for the right reasons.

Our biggest problems arise through relationships and so it is through relationships that we discover ourselves, learning tolerance, understanding that love is an energy we all must share in equal parts until we can truly participate in the purest form of all love, compassion. Eventually our apprenticeship will be over and we will become Masters in our own right.

Everything in and around the Earth is motivated by feelings of one kind or another and learning to deal with many situations with a limited amount of resources is extremely difficult. The choices we make create the world about us, create our future and create our spiritual growth and the choice is all ours.

Here we have a very limited time span in which to accomplish pre determined achievements. We exist in a very dense physical body with limited movements often giving us a limited overview of what is possible elsewhere. The physical body is robot liked compared to other planes and planets, comparatively stiff with far fewer resources. The computer like brain is absolutely essential for the upkeep of the body and whilst is has been programmed to retain control of the health and well being of the body, it is a fragile structure about which as yet we know all too little.

Outside of the physical programme it oversees, it acts as an interpreter for Mind via the thoughts that bombard it, creating a warehouse for those thoughts we decide to keep hold of, our memory banks.

The Earth plane for example is where we are now. We are conscious it is a very physical world. It can be a very colourful world, a very noisy world teeming with different life forms, each getting on with their lives in their own different ways but within this world there is also seemingly a fine disregard for human life and all other life forms by the human species. There is a pecking order, a superiority of man over the animals, the insects, the plants and vegetation and within the races of man also. This makes for a world that is always at war with one or another of its species that tells us a great deal about where we are in the scheme of things.

We rarely attribute other qualities to this world in a way that we should. We either ignore the sublime and the ethereal or create superstitions always bordering on gothic horror – man's worst nightmares. So we never get in touch with Earth itself, attuning to its finer aspects, glorying in its ethereal beauty, recognising it as Healer, Artist extraordinaire and a Teller of Tales.

Instead man tends to keep his sights and therefore his perceptions firmly on solid ground. But the Earth is surrounded by it's own energy fields just as we are. These energy fields are connected directly to planes of existence just as real as the Earth plane and as solid as the physical is in their own way. Life on these planes have much more substance and are stepping stones to the future, leading us ever onwards to the Source.

The Astral Plane

The subtle differences between the astral and the physical dimensions are truly only a step away but the difference in resources is immense. Being or living on the astral plane is a different matter altogether. There, there is the opportunity to learn and grow emotionally, mentally and spiritually, as we are much more in control. There is in many ways less pressure and more 'time'. Much of what the people of Earth 'discover' is first explored and experimented with on the astral. There is a true awareness of our creating our own realities and the results of such thinking, such creation, is again a growth process.

People are just as real there as people are here. There is no apparent difference. They still look the same although they can choose to alter their appearances. Those who have been there for some time may appear taller, slimmer, have more hair etc. It is simply a matter of personal preference. There is matter and water and colour and plants and trees and animals but of course time wears a different coat. There are objectives and aims, goals to be met but on the astral it will take as long as your interest and effort make it. The same form is used but the need for internal organs is no longer there. Depending on the level of attainment of the individual, personal excesses will be eliminated. There is no need for food because life is sustained automatically but one can eat or drink simply because one wishes to until it is realised that it isn't necessary for the sustenance of the form they occupy. There is no need to walk but they do because it is natural whilst still in a recognizable form to behave in some ways as they did whilst in the physical body.

We can see ourselves close up and further away at the same time. It is a strange experience in which we may find ourselves being in the subjective situation as well as being the objective observer if we have gone there to learn a particular lesson. We can actually see ourselves as others see us.

We do not have the same need to use the sense of smell as there is no appetite to whet but in other more subtle ways we can 'smell the roses'. We can sit and read as one might on earth or we can simply look 'through' the book without turning a page. There are different reasons for doing either one or the other.

It is the same with animals and flowers and trees. The next plane is not completely different from earth. It is just as real and solid in the next plane as it is here but there is more. There are houses and countryside, flowers and rivers, churches and temples. Not a lot changes because people haven't changed that much. Their creations in both worlds are very similar.

As there is no need to have sexual intercourse in order to produce children, acts surrounding sexual activity are unnecessary, simply a mechanical means to an end on Earth, which here are no longer needed. That doesn't mean that physical love is prohibited. Instead, a love shared is expressed by a deeply satisfying 'blending' experience as the two bodies come close which is far more sensuous and 'orgasmic' than anything that occurs whilst in the physical body. It will only happen when two people want it to unlike experiences in the physical world where there may be much pretence and very little desire for one party. Just as telepathy means no lies, the desire and or the love have to be real. Genuine affection may be shown by a hug or a kiss just the same and one can still take a walk down a country lane, hand in hand listening to the sounds of the countryside.

People may speak to each other or catch each other's thoughts, although communication by telepathy is not always used. Those who still prefer to speak may do so but those more highly evolved will automatically use telepathy. It is much faster and direct, thoughts flashing between people, leaving no room for misunderstandings. But thoughts used in this way are not silent thoughts, as one would imagine them to be, presupposing a silent world.

Sound is everywhere; we just appreciate it in a different way. The astral form encompasses many other receptors around the form as well as the organs of eyes and ears. These receptors are not visible but are an integral part of the astral makeup. One can appreciate good music never before heard in this way, beautiful in every detail, voices singing in many different harmonies at the same time, truly out of this world. Art visualised from the front and back at the same time create amazing pictures, four, five or six dimensional. Colours you cannot begin to imagine vibrating at the level of energy they represent. Pulsing and moving shades in perpetual motion constantly enlarging and reducing the size bringing the picture to life, a real life of its own with sound as an option. Nothing is flat, colourless or static. Another can add to the scene and the work exists for all time. Those who love the fine arts in this way, spend much time where imagination is limitless and creativity endless.

We are in many ways very similar, as we are here but much freer in mind and body. There is an upliftment there because fear does not rule. The difference between here and there is palpable. The fear around this plane is heavy like treacle, dense and wearing, like being held in an iron grip from which one is forever struggling to be a 'free spirit' in more ways than one.

There is so much we can tap into, so much we can experience away from the Earth plane, one should never worry about 'What comes Next.'

The Mental Plane

The mental energy fields are required in every dimension including the astral, naturally, but there is a mental plane where we can go to work things through without the colourful emotional field getting in the way, obstructing the real view.

Marjorie Sutton

The mental level is more logical and on this level we can learn to see things more clearly without reflecting our emotional states and those of others. On the mental plane we can work things out much more quickly as we need to due to the time schedule the physical world has. When we are still living on Earth we have to operate at the slowest beat.

If we work solely in the mental field when we leave the body to work within the mental dimension or on the mental plane we may not always have form. Again one can see and understand physical beings but all communication is through mental processes including telepathy. The Self remains true. Nothing can diminish it. Because the emotional fields are not there, the personality does not always come across. The true Self or Spirit is complete and as Self is both male and female, contact by the Self to a person in the physical world could come across as one or the other or, as just an impression.

On the mental plane there is form but the thought processes are used constantly, rationalising, working through problems without the constraints the emotional side brings to a situation. Here, when out of body we can enact what is going on in our earth lives in order to put it right. Seeing the situation for what it is without the glamour of love and duty, religious fervour or political might. Understanding that beyond the earthly desires there are factors which must not be denied and we can return to our daily lives with that new understanding. On earth this often comes as a flash of 'intuition' and can change the direction of an individual or a nation.

The Plane of Preparation

One of the planes is that of Preparation. Here, people work as they might in laboratories and factories on Earth except of course that on this plane it is a true labour of love. They don't just create something, they try many different variations on a theme taking into account all the necessary information they have about life on Earth as it is and as it will be say, in fifty years time. People's desires as well as their needs are taken into account for the need will be overlooked if the desire for something else is greater. Man doesn't often seem to get his priorities right and this is recognised and acknowledge elsewhere also.

One cannot relate time there to time here but about ten years ago I was shown an aeroplane, which was white, huge, and had a triangular shape to the main body as well as the overall design. Inside, the rows of seats grew in length as it spread towards the rear, rising slightly as seats in a theatre might. At the rear was a staircase leading to a bar in the balcony above, a refreshment area and a gallery of some kind where people could stretch their legs and have a chat. At the front of the plane was a large screen for viewing videos throughout the flight. It seemed to be flown from the rear and not the front as we see planes today. The whole design was completely different to anything to be seen today but then I don't know what people are working on here behind their hangar doors.

One of the problems with man up to and at the present time is that when great discoveries are made, if there can be a vested interest, the needs of Nature and Man are abandoned. Instead, devious minds look at how they can thwart the Eternal Plan for petty personal gain. This will never ultimately come to pass but in the human experiments much harm is done to both humans and animals. There have been breakthroughs in a number of departments but man cannot see any further than his nose. One example is cloning. We are assured that this is OK so that we can create ourselves knowing very little at this stage about the energy fields of man and animals. Without that knowledge, man is not going very far. The two cannot be separated. One reason for organ rejection is due to the different energy fields of those concerned, not gelling. Cloning we are told amongst other things will provide organs for man which will help the suffering. DNA and identifying genes. There are far more vested interests with the commercial side of these discoveries than with the simple notion of help for all mankind. Man always seems to go off at a tangent and this too is taken into account by those in the celestial workshops and laboratories. Man is the most dangerous of all the animal kingdom. Not the many, just the few but the few with the power.

But in many practical ways people on this plane are also working to make life more beautiful on what was once a truly beautiful planet. One way or another man will have to see the errors of his ways before these projects manifest on Earth but they will.

As for cures for ills, man has to learn more about himself and in doing that learn about prevention. He has also to learn to look in many different directions if he seeks to alleviate pain and disease. Those on the plane of preparation are working on the principles of being able to work through the dimensions. In other words, they are looking towards helping us more from their planes but that is all energy work. In order for anyone to operate on a different level there has to be a difference in individual vibrations. These vibrations have to come together and gel in order to get close to another in another dimension. They work in the etheric fields as do all energy workers here, healers and such like.

I was recently shown many technical plans to advance the work within energy fields from their and our level but until science accepts and acknowledges not just the electro magnetic field around the human form but the subtler fields also, that is very much for the future. Scientists must learn to look at life and death differently if they are to move on. The commercial operations must also view the suffering more and the share prices less.

Holistically, the whole being is equally important. The planet is full of natural aids often chopped down and thrown away, there being no commercial value or chopped up and ending up as toilet rolls. Governments seem to be in love with commercialism and personal gain is rife in every country on Earth. Money is always found for wars whether people are starving through lack of help from their own or from others, so it is in this three dimensional world and illness is not given the priority it should be. There are too many hidden agendas and vested interests and until man learns to grow spiritually a little more the mass of the people will continue to suffer.

It has nothing to do with any God. It has everything to do with personal responsibility that man has towards his fellow man and to the planet Earth. The answers are here but the people are not asking the right questions. There is too much wasted trust between those who have not and those who have. All it will take is for every person to remember they are part of a team and that no matter how rich or how famous, alone, they are going nowhere in the true scheme of things. Thankfully these matters do not stop those elsewhere from working towards future goals to ensure that when the time is right, when man is right, much will be available to him.

There are of course many people who are excellent mediums and clairvoyants and there are many very genuine healers on Earth at the moment. These are all people who have chosen to work in this way and when we say that the best are born with these abilities it is true. Our energy fields or chakra system shows our development in certain areas. This applies to all people whether they are great writers, artists, singers, sportspersons or scientists. Particular aspects of the energy fields are already developed at birth. This does not mean that people cannot develop as they go along but for those who need to work in a particular way as part of their destiny, the means are available to them from the word go. It may be some time later in life when they are able to take on the role of mediators, spiritually, as they may also have other matters to attend to first but the best have always had that ability from birth.

Those in the spiritual arena use the connections that are open to them for communication for any sort of prophecy or far viewing via the energy fields so it is a very natural thing to do. It shouldn't be seen as 'phenomena'. Neither should it be seen as a gift from God. People have worked hard to earn the so-called gifts of the Spirit and have chosen to use them in their present incarnation.

Sadly some of these very bright prospects become lazy, making money for only the minimum of effort and as such the communication is basic to say the least. Others never stop developing their abilities and work very hard at their communication skills. No one however can be in contact with another who is far beyond him or her in terms of spiritual development and this is truly shown in the communications they convey.

Some have the ability to see what has gone on, on the plane of reparation and can help to a certain extent, people in need here. In other realms, symbols are often used as graphical reinforcement. Here too, many symbols are used and here is where misinterpretation often takes place. Not with the best but with those who believe they have a 'gift' when all they have is a small amount of psychic ability. For those working at the highest levels it is possible for them to work, they are usually very self-critical always seeking the best for their clients by hard work and serious development projects. Being a 'natural' doesn't mean that you cannot improve.

When the time is appropriate for someone to advance in their role as mediators, there is much activity during the sleep and meditation states, which is why meditation is so important. These are the times when it is easier for those they have a connection with, to make contact or to adjust their energy fields accordingly to bring the different dimensions closer. There is no question of Mr Joe Bloggs suddenly becoming a healer or a medium and certainly not working with higher beings within two days of reading a book!

This can take many lifetimes of gradual progression and the more advanced people here also work within other dimensions with those same higher beings. In this way their energy fields are aligned from the outset and the contact can become as simple as people here talking to each other.

The men of science working within the energy field programme on the plane of preparation also have mediators on Earth who are capable of working in a particular way with others from other dimensions. This needs refining and those here need to know more about the processes than they do at the present time. Again one cannot simply show someone or a group a particular ritual in order to work with someone from another realm. It just isn't that easy, again because of the difference in energy fields.

Everything elsewhere appears to have a singularly pleasing appropriateness about it. People on the level which is best for them, teachers and mentors always available to them and the Collective Mind promoting levels of creativity and purpose in a seeming Utopia. Travelling is easy, for to think of someone or some place quickly brings it to fruition. There is all the time one needs to think, work something out, experiment and meet with these mentors and advisors - if one is there full time of course. And people do spend inordinate amounts of time in creating future projects with the Earth in mind. However, there has to be a certain synchronicity. It wouldn't work for someone to come up with a bright idea and simply bring it through to Earth. Everything has to be at the right time, bearing everything in mind that is going on on Earth at that time and for the foreseeable future.

As individuals we create our own futures here, by every decision we take every day. Collectively the group soul is evolving at it's own pace within it's own set parameters over a time span of decades which in turn span millenniums. Whilst the ultimate outcome will come about through the Will of the Creator, all the choices we can make ensures that *when* this will happen is a cosmically unknown factor. Nothing is set in stone. Nevertheless hope springs eternal and plans for the future go on a pace.

After a number of Council Meetings with all the interested parties, certain individuals do come to Earth to further our progress as a race. We have seen this with all the Masters and the great Men of Science and the Arts throughout the centuries and so it will continue.

The Plane of Reparation

Here we can learn how to make amends but not only that. We can also be shown why things are going wrong in relationships and we can be brought together to discuss not just amongst ourselves but with other members of the group soul who have a vested interest in us getting it right for all concerned both here and there. We all have to get it right and the first step in any problematic relationship is in understanding. Visits to this plane show us how we are able to see how it really is/was, not just for us but for others too. We have to look at thoughts, words and deeds and the intentions surrounding them.

On Earth there is so much going on that we often do not listen to others or believe others or see any further than our own desires, ignoring all the warning signs along the way. On this plane we can see a clearer picture and we can be shown all the steps which were taken to create that picture. We can be shown that we, not the others are wrong sometimes. It isn't just a question of being told. The interested parties are taken to that plane and can enact the present but with a difference. No lies. People are encouraged gently to listen to what is being said by another and they are shown what is behind a person's motivation so that they can understand fully the other's point of view. It is not a question of apportioning blame but of taking back responsibility for their own part in the play. It is very much about equality.

Whereas here one person may be the stronger, there everyone is equal. *They all read the same script.* They remember what their purpose or role is here and they can look very objectively at all the twists and turns they and others have taken which have perhaps resulted in changing the play for the worse. Sometimes we are shown things symbolically, which is a very powerful tool used correctly. It is quicker than discussion or enactment. Our time is always at a premium and the method is not always foolproof. The symbols have to be interpreted correctly. For example, I was in a situation with another lady who despite protestations of love for her partner was in fact making herself ill. No amount of talking or listening could make her see what the problem was. One night we found ourselves along with her partner on this plane of reparation. He had had a number of affairs. She had convinced herself that she had forgiven, there was no animosity, and it was all in the past. Her partner held his ground over one relationship which was affecting the present very seriously. He spoke gently but firmly about the feelings he had for this person which were not feelings of a sexual nature but of respect and of paying off a moral debt. He was simply helping someone who had in the past helped him.

Marjorie Sutton

One of the things shown to her was herself, symbolically, as a skeleton with a huge padlock and chain around her pelvic girdle. She was terribly shocked but finally understood that she hadn't quite dealt with the past however many years ago it was. Realising this, she was able to get the help she needed instead of going into denial. Although symbolic it was an actual representation of what was going on in her life.

On another occasion a male friend who had taken a particular role in the play had gone astray during his lifetime, becoming embittered and revengeful and therefore unable to undertake the challenges which were about to present themselves. His ability to play the role was crucial for a number of the other players but he was only interested in opting out. Despite a number of outings to that plane and a 'recovery' programme set up for him on that plane, he still opted out which was and still is a major problem for that particular group soul.

It is a wonderful opportunity that is allowed to us but it is of course done during the sleep state here and when we awaken we either have altered our views or we have not. We are not *made* to see the truth of the matter. As always everything must come from within. To this end, when we are at a crucial point in our lives, we may visit this plane on a number of occasions, leaving no stone unturned in our efforts to get it right.

There are times on Earth when, in a crisis people begin to have doubts about future plans or they may begin to see people a little differently, not quite believing how the change has come about or how they could change their opinion so completely about another. This is probably why. People should always follow their hunches, their gut reactions, that thing we call women's intuition or our sixth sense. These are all remnants of our psychic inheritance and will always serve us true. All of us have the ability to tap into the Collective Mind or to contact our higher self through a natural inbuilt connection via the energy fields.

When we have passed from this life we are able to go to this plane and learn the ways in which we can make true reparation. We are shown what is happening to people on Earth. We can see what is going to happen and how we can help people to either avoid a situation altogether or to help them through what has to be.

Not surprisingly, many are amazed to see themselves as they really are and after they have got over the shock they have to set about putting it right or as right as they can. We are all guilty of many mistakes, downright lies, improper behaviour, cheating on our fellow man and like all children we think we are clever enough to get away with it. But the cosmic video doesn't lie nor does it miss anything, which is just as well because we are not all bad and many good things we have done have probably been forgotten by us.

There comes a time when we are ready to have a look at our latest life with our mentors and work out just what is needed to make reparation. Again we have free choice and those on the lower levels of evolution often opt for the status quo, reincarnating again and again without making very much progress which is why so many workers are required to work in these areas to bring about an advancement of those group souls. There is no apathy or complacency there and just like many here, they put their heads down and just get on with the work, seeking no recognition outside that of those they seek to advance.

Those who are seriously trying to help mankind simply because there is a need will eventually triumph. On Earth the news is always about the negative because it is usually sensational. We must never forget that the positive is going on too. If we all contribute, like all light, it will disperse the darkness.

One of the most important aspects of the whole concept of reparation is that those who are wishing to make reparation are allowed to do so!

Have you been terribly hurt, lost a loved one in dreadful circumstances, suffered abuse…the list is endless and the person who caused all this is wishing to make amends. Sometimes it is so very difficult to allow this in as much as the hurt goes deep and all you want is for that person to suffer over and over again. That is understandable and this in itself can take more than one lifetimes to allow it, until we can bear even the thought of that person in anything but the role of evil.

Personal responsibility can never be taken away. Reparation has always to be made for even the smallest hurt or pain we have caused another. It is far far better, easier and quicker in the long run to make reparation whilst in the same plane of existence. How much easier to meet, discuss, try to see the other person's point of view, allow that feelings change, people change and agree to let people go without animosity. Holding onto hurt only hurts you in many ways. Trying to understand may take some time, making reparation or allowing someone else to may take longer but in the end it is truly worth it.

When people die and leave without having first made reparation it is much harder to do so from another plane but it can be done. Although no one can alter a person's life experiences or make things right through a quick fix solution, there are ways and means that people can help from elsewhere within set parameters. It isn't the easiest way but it can be done – with the person's consent! The person who has been hurt must agree to allow that person to make amends.

Sometimes, the love and the need to make amends is so great that despite extraordinary progress being made by an individual after returning, they will stay behind to ensure a particular person's safety or help in some way with their progression on earth. Sacrifices are made on other planes too, sacrifices that however hurt one has been, one wouldn't want to inflict on another. But when people do see the error of their ways they are truly mortified and they will spend all their time trying to help as much as it is possible, the ones on Earth they have harmed. Because of this it is very important to either not think of those who have harmed you or to send out your thoughts to them allowing them to make reparation for it is amazing when this is done, how they can benefit you. The worst thing one can do is to send hate and bitterness out. It serves no purpose at all and only brings that person down to the level of the offender. It usually makes the person ill and doesn't alter anything. There is a natural sense of injustice and there are genuine feelings of outrage at some acts committed here. The best possible way is to act constructively so that these things do not happen to others. In this way the energy spent will be doing a great deal of good instead of a great deal of harm, especially to the Self.

However, we mercifully don't remember past incarnations and the damage we too may have caused another but again, thankfully, we have been allowed to make reparation and move on. It is not the same as forgiveness. Similar but very different too. In forgiveness-not in words but from the heart- *we* have to let things go. In reparation *they* have to do all the work, changing *their* views on what is acceptable and what is not and that change will never alter once made. The gross can become honed in time and the more we allow this, give them permission to atone usually through helping the ones they have hurt, the quicker the species of man will come through into the Light.

A Meeting with Spiritual Mentors

There is no spiritual plane as such, as spirit operates in and permeates everywhere but there are higher realms or planes where the more evolved work. These may be called our spiritual mentors. Higher beings who despite being more advanced have opted to stay close to help those who are less evolved. When traveling to these higher planes I have found that I always have a companion to ensure that I arrive safely.

The first time it happened it came as quite a shock. After my experiences over a number of years working in and around the earth plane on one plane or another, in one dimension or another, helping others in this life and those who had passed over, I awoke to find myself surrounded by a myriad of colour and the sound as if of a thousand crisp packets in my ears. I hadn't experienced this before and immediately questioned what was happening. Something very special was about to, of that I had no doubt. I immediately asked 'Who was there, what was happening?' I was told that I was to go out to the higher spiritual realms and for this I needed a protector. Someone who could shield me from the stronger vibrations to be found in these higher dimensions – the bridge between the lower and the higher worlds. For a second I wasn't sure but if this were something bad I would go anyway, I had no control over it and if it was good, it would be fantastic. I asked them to always in future, ask my permission before taking me, needing to feel that I had a say in matters. Control freak? Foolish perhaps but it wasn't just a gut reaction. In future I would need to know the format, the familiar.

They confirmed that they would and darkness followed. In what seemed seconds I found myself in a country like place where people were involved in conversation. As always there was a sense of beauty, an ambience of calm where one immediately felt amongst trusted friends. Of the half a dozen people waiting for me, two of them were very tall men and another was tiny. This small man was a very old and a very wise Chinese gentleman wearing the clothes worn in the days of the Chinese Emperors. I recognised him immediately. He was my philosophy mentor. He was called Cheng. He always showed himself as Chinese calling me 'little missy'. We had been together for aeons of time. Before this I had received many writings from him, full of wisdom, great teachings. I used to think his teachings were just for me as I could always relate to them when certain things were happening in my life until one day, someone came to me with a problem and I immediately thought of one of these teachings. I then realised that true wisdom applies to everyone and every situation.

There was an aura of red around and after we had greeted each other I was informed that I was to be shown the answer to my recent questions on trance mediumship. I had been wondering for a long time about the practicalities of such an event and asking how much of the approaching spirit actually contacted the physical body of the medium. Whilst one can be aware of a presence being very close there was always talk of communicators 'taking over' the medium. I hadn't thought this possible, as the spirit has to work within set parameters within the medium's energy fields. There were so many seemingly silly things said on the subject that I wanted confirmation of the reality of it, if it did exist at all.

In the background was a large beautiful horse in many shades of red. I knew from this that the lesson would be concerned with strong magnetic energy fields. I asked Cheng now if that was what I was about to learn. He nodded and replied that it was. Immediately, as I watched, the horse seemed to come very close, partially entering my energy fields from the head to the waist, the back half of it remaining outside my body. I couldn't see the front half of the horse and for some reason I was immediately incensed, not liking the thought of an animal so close to me, I suppose.

But Cheng held his ground and explained to me that the horse represented strength – spiritual strength and that a spirit could use a medium by getting this close energywise, for communication to take place. So basically, someone could come close, convey their message by voice using the medium's voice box and vocal chords and then move away when the message was over. It seemed to be about energy transference. As the spiritual vibration is quite different, it wouldn't really be able to affect the physical in the way that people had understood it but on a physics level, the two were quite different. The medium would of necessity come out of body partially or wholly because the more highly evolved, more knowable and therefore more safe spiritual communicator could do the job.

This could happen too with healing when an evolved being could work within the energy fields of another but in that instance; the healer/spirit would go out of body thus allowing a clear field for energy transference by someone who knew what they were doing. This seems to be the case with those working with those who some call spirit doctors. It is rare because the energy fields have to be finely tuned to both healer and Spiritual helper in order for this type of bonding to take place.

I recognised the symbolism of the horse and the entry but still, I was so angry. I couldn't feel the horse inside me at all, there was no physical awareness as it had all been symbolic but for some reason I thought it could have been done better. When it was time to leave I was given a plaque by Cheng of a three dimensional red/bronze sculpting of the head and shoulders of a horse. I didn't want to take it but he held it out to me and I took it very reluctantly, really not wanting it. I don't know where my anger came from and I told them not to come for me again. And they didn't. Not for ten years! By this time of course I had come to my senses, realising much later that they had only done as I had asked them to do months before in my search for the truth. And they had done it beautifully but in my own small awareness I had behaved very badly.

Months later when light dawned I apologised for my spiritual immaturity but I had to accept that they may never help me again in this way until and unless I grew up. They were far too busy to make all that effort to come for me and take me to a very special place just to communicate with me. They certainly wouldn't put me under pressure. After all it was my need not theirs. It was very disappointing for me and I could have kicked myself. As the years went by I began to think that I would never go out again or meet with my spiritual mentors in this way. I knew that I probably didn't deserve it. I had been too precious by far.

A few years later I returned from a long flight and went straight to bed for a few hours. I set my alarm as I had an appointment to keep and when the alarm rang I came to but I wasn't completely in sync. The walls of my bedroom were bevelled just like a house might be portrayed in a Disney movie. In fact it reminded me of the house in the film 'The Seven Dwarfs'. The wood of my wardrobes was a beautiful pulsating brown, the wallpaper a luminescent pale green and as I looked around me, delighted with this fairy like room my attention was caught by a plaque on the wall. Since my last meeting on the higher spiritual planes I had moved my bed to another position in the room. But over where the bedhead used to be was the plaque that Cheng had given me upon my leaving that higher plane all those years before. A plaque of the head and shoulders of the red/bronze horse. The strength and the spiritual love had always been there. Despite my own reluctant acceptance of this, their very special gift to me, it had hung there ever since that night and I had never known.

It hadn't been taken from me and I marvelled at their patience. They had taken me at my word in my anger and in trust they had kept away. They had given a great deal of time to me to learn and repent at leisure not to punish me but in order for me to know that I could always trust them to do what I asked them to. They would never and have never done anything against my wishes. Betrayal was not in their nature.

I have been extremely privileged to meet my mentors whilst still in the physical body and remember it. So much happens which we do not remember for very good reason. The pain would truly be excruciating if we could recall all our meetings with the ones we hold so dear. Being here would be hell on earth knowing the ones we leave behind are a part of us. As it is most people are completely unaware of those elsewhere whose love means more to them than can possibly be expressed in human terms. Forgetting is a luxury they afford us to help us remain here until our work is done.

Very often when we are ready to progress a little further and we have the ability to venture out, we are asked to take on the role of counsellor to those in darker realms. For this too we are accompanied by a spiritual mentor to protect and teach us. The memories of these encounters are definitely not remembered more than once because some things that are witnessed are so distressing. For me I found a correlation with my work here at the time and I realised how and where my abhorence of pedophiles originated. Many people find them an abomination but my feelings go further than that and I can see no foreseeable time when my views will alter. For me they are at a very basic level, gross. The excesses perpetrated here are a true reflection of another plane and so much work still is required.

When working in this capacity I was always met and taught by the man who was chief mentor in the healing work I had undertaken from childhood and working with those who relished their gross excesses always left me feeling sick on my return here. I have learned and matured enough to do the work now on my own but those are memories I can do without and mercifully they have been withheld.

Marjorie Sutton

Visitors

Sometimes work has to be done with us whilst we are still around the physical realms and our mentors have to visit us here in our own setting to show us what is around us or to work within our energy fields and even to operate on the physical body. It is perhaps important to recognise here that advanced beings cannot work with one who has not reached a certain level because they would blow the energy fields. There has to be an attunement one with another so that the balance is kept and we are not harmed. Any notion that it can happen anytime to anyone is false.

One night I awoke to find that I could not move, I was surrounded by the blackest of black and the feeling of strength so strong it was truly frightening. There were no beautiful colours or sounds of electrical static or winds to herald a trip out. This time it was as if I was locked in a vice on my bed. I wondered what I should do, then realised there was nothing I could do. Just relax I told myself. Everything will be OK. If what is here is not good, there's nothing I can do about it. Let's just go with the flow, my friends will be around somewhere, I am not alone and if I don't relax I may never see who it is. 'OK' I said mentally, 'I'm ready'. Immediately the room lightened and although I could not see anyone I knew that whoever were there, were on my side. The power they had brought with them was just overwhelming. They explained that they needed to know the balance of my energy fields and to give me more energy in this dimension, on this plane. I stepped out of body for a few seconds whilst they decided to experiment with the energy fields. It was all to do with how long I could remain out of body without harming my nervous system apparently.

I watched as the form on the bed was surrounded by a most wonderful silver light that wrapped itself around my physical body and the bed. As it spun round me, an almost solid, tangible energy field was being built up or reharmonised as I waited. Then I was asked if I would go out very close to my home as they wanted to teach me something whilst I was waiting. I agreed and found myself flying, a little like Peter Pan, above the house and into nearby countryside. I looked down at one point to see the figure of a woman, a young woman suspended it would seem from a tree. Not hanging but suspended from a branch in a very similar way. She wore a long white robe, she had blonde shoulder length curly hair and her eyes were wide open. I stopped and looked at her but she showed no sign of life. I wondered what I was being shown. Think about it I was told. I did.

I looked all around me. It was nightime and the tree was in the astral dimension. Although it was summer in real time this tree had no leaves and the top branch was broken like a pointing finger. Was the figure meant to represent me? Was I stuck in my thinking? Was I going to commit suicide? Was someone I knew going to commit suicide? I didn't think so but then, what do I know. I moved around the figure again. What feeling did I get? Well, she wasn't moving, she wasn't seeing and she should be able to move off from there because there was no attachment of any kind, physical or astral to keep her there. So why was she there?

It was time to go on, this time to a hospital where I watched an operation being performed but before I could move on in closer to see if I knew them, I could feel my weight returning and I had to return immediately to my room. There was some technical talk going on amongst my friends that I did not understand or even try to but more changes had to be made this time with me back in the physical body. I did as I was told and once more had the pleasure of being wrapped in silver for quite some time. Then it was time for them to go. They returned each night for almost a week checking the vibrations but no more adventures for me.

A few months later as winter embraced us, I was driving to a friend's house out of town down a road I often use when I had to stop in order to allow cattle to pass. This had never happened before and as I looked up at the surrounding trees, now bare of all leaves I saw *that* tree, the one I had seen with the young woman suspended from it. The broken branch was pointing to the far side of the road just a few yards away. On the side of the road I could see flowers growing, unusual in a wild hedgerow and then I remembered. There had been a fatal accident there earlier in the year and her family had made a shrine almost of the place where it happened. They were keeping her memory in such a way that she couldn't get on with her new life. They must have been grief-stricken, unable to let go and their beautiful daughter was being bombarded by their thoughts and their grief. She was not an 'earthbound' spirit but they were not helping her by letting go, wishing her well and allowing her to adjust to her new life.

Knowing how much those left behind suffer is not easy for anyone who has returned. The whole scene whilst in the astral dimension, was having a bad effect on this place. They had created a place for her here where she did not wish to be, completely without their knowing but their thoughts had been so focused and negative that she was constantly made aware of the earth instead of getting on with her life, her work elsewhere in peace and happiness.

It is so important to let go, for everybody's sake. That doesn't mean forget but they should instead try to entertain only those memories that celebrated her life, recognizing their own blessings in having had the privilege of living with her for however many years. I felt so sad for the family for whom it had all been too much and were suffering still. The shrine was a token of their love but it was their negative thoughts and sorrow that would reach her and there was nothing she could do about it.

There is so much unnecessary material like this in the dimensions around the Earth plane that interferes with the energy fields and their vibrations, creating blockages which in themselves can do harm. It is good to think of those who have gone but with love and laughter and a sense of adventure and a knowing that one day you will meet up again and what a lot you will have to say!

Pre Life Agreements, Karma and Reincarnation

The concepts of Pre life agreements, karma and reincarnation need to be studied in order to make any sense at all of life here, there and everywhere.

Trying to understand consciousness can be hard going at first for even the most intelligent of people because it begs many, many questions so often never explored. In answering those questions, sometimes the scaffolding we have surrounded ourselves with has to be slowly removed and another set of safety guards erected. For many it is easier to close the door on thinking and take the road of the 'just enjoy, after all we only have one life, let's live it to the full' brigade. It is a popular notion. It is also an illusion, it doesn't alter reality. For those who prefer this attitude it often helps them cope with the experiences they encounter here whereby they are very often doing amazing things in order to make their mark in this 'one life'.

On the other hand, others with this view see only a pointlessness and blackness of outlook forever that sends them in a very different direction. Sometimes it becomes that of evil and control or a downward spiral of apathy and despair. However, for the sincere seeker of truth it is always a question of pushing back boundaries, exploring new territories, seeing with new eyes so that whatever the conclusions, people will know they have taken their own voyage of discovery and found their truth for themselves.

We are given a number of packages during the course of a lifetime each of them a direction to another package and within each package there is a mystery to be solved before we can travel further. It is only by opening the package, solving the mystery and journeying on, that enlightenment will come. Expanding our knowledge in this way serves a fourfold purpose. Firstly, we take control of our own destiny by planning the route we are to take. Secondly, we learn about other cultures and creeds each of them a signpost to a different spiritual adventure, each of them concealing the truth within the elaborate packaging. Thirdly, we can tolerate another's viewpoint even if we do not accept it for ourselves, understanding that many roads lead to Universal knowledge. Fourthly, we can say… *I know*, because *I* have taken the journey.

In **Pre life agreements,** we see the picture as it presents before we are born, for only the physical form begins here. The spiritual intelligence which will inhabit and use that form whilst on Earth is already alive and kicking elsewhere and very often has been for aeons of time. People often ponder on where we go to after death but not very often, on where we come from before our physical birth. As we will see, the two places are the same. The place of origin will vary depending on the evolution of the soul or group soul but similar projects are carried out on whatever level that happens to be.

Many people talk about the soul and there are many variations on a theme as to what the soul is or where it is. Different religions have different views. Individuals are often called 'souls' and we all understand the term as it is applied on Earth. Whatever one's view is, it is important not to get too specific because the concept of a soul esoterically viewed would promote much interesting discussion without actually formulating a definite image. I would prefer to keep it as simple as it needs to be to understand the message.

We are all members of a **Group Soul** in order to learn and grow not only spiritually but also physically, emotionally and mentally. We have to experience many things. Whatever the individual learns through experience, the group soul benefits from. It is like this. Take a large bucket of clear water (group soul). Next, remove a few drops of that water (individuals) and place them in particular situations, each situation being represented here by a dye. After a period, bring the drops of water back into the bucket. The dyes will thus colour the water, all the water. Thus, the group soul benefits from every individual experience. Thus, when people incarnate on Earth, the whole of the group soul is not always involved but they will benefit from those incarnations. Therefore, there may be people working on another plane who could be a soulmate or a twin soul who one forgets whilst experiencing life here but who is waiting for you to return at the appropriate time.

Pre-life agreements determine the roles we all commit to for our next incarnation. We along with other members of the Group Soul, Spiritual Mentors and Advisors write the script for the **Play**. We choose our role which means that we choose particular situations, challenges and goals in an attempt to further our own and others spiritual advancement.

Sometimes we are the central figure within the Play, sometimes it is only a walk on role. Some find themselves having a 'bit' part in a number of Plays acting as a catalyst. The roles are many and varied, the characters diverse, the length of the Play may extend into generations or the run may be short.

Not everyone who comes into our life here, in the Play is part of our group soul and whilst we may be close to people here it doesn't always follow that they are the closest to us elsewhere. It doesn't matter. Being close to another here is part of the Play and here, the Play is all that matters. The Play is the product of the Pre-life agreements we have made, agreed and rubber stamped by us.

We live on Earth to experience the experience and the Play allows us to have that experience. Like all Plays, there is a plot, there are characters that bring challenges or support, and there is an outcome. The **Roles** we play depend on the experiences, challenges, and knowledge we need in order to grow spiritually. It is all a learning process associated with growth. As individuals, we have to experience many things in many ways and we do this by taking different roles each time we incarnate.

Marjorie Sutton

Within this Role-Play, our greatest adversary could be a soulmate; one who has agreed to work with us on Earth to support us in often very difficult and dangerous situations as a measure of their love for us. They could be Playing devil's advocate and the better they play their part the more we learn. Matters are often the very opposite of what they seem here, soulmates presenting a very different face but they are just playing their part. On the other hand, we may incarnate and spend our life with a soulmate, happy, sharing caring and learning together. We should see the Play for what it is.

The Play is only a part of our reality and when our role is finished, the time for our exit arrives and we leave the stage and go home. It is important to recognise that people are coming and going all the time and we must play our part the very best we can in order to keep the Play going. If we decide to change parts or opt out all together, we leave others high and dry and can change the Play significantly, losing the plot and therefore the outcome. Sometimes another will step in and try to keep the Play going. Everything depends on the circumstances at the time.

There are those who have not incarnated whose jobs are to keep a close eye on things so that whenever possible, contingency plans can be put into action. Just as here we have producers, directors, designers and the props so do we have a similar team albeit elsewhere, working hard throughout the Play to ensure the best outcome for everyone.

Sometimes the Play falls down due to people deviating from the script. Despite a great deal of effort, compromise and adaptability from the team upstairs, all does not always go to plan. Perhaps a specific duo is fulfilling karma and pursuing their destinies. If they break down, the opportunity is lost.

When great destiny is involved, there is often a great deal of activity on the astral plane with all the Players to keep it on course. During out of body meetings, discussions are held with other members of the group soul and spiritual mentors, to try and get both parties to work together, reminding them of their reason d'être.

It usually means that people do continue together on Earth but not always. When one of the party insists on leaving it isn't just traumatic in the physical world it is consequential elsewhere. The problem is of course that most people do not remember these meetings on the astral or their agreements when they take up consciousness in the physical body again.

Paradoxically, there are those who insist on staying together when their experiences together and their destinies or karma have been fulfilled. It is time for them to move on, leaving both of them free to go to the next stage in different Plays or perhaps they are playing a bit part in other peoples Plays but they never make it.

This is one of a number of reasons why people have to keep reincarnating. Getting it wrong means having to have another go, in another time, and another place.

Society in different cultures create problems by their rules and regulations based only on mans' own notions and whimsies which change over the years and the centuries. This accounts for the confusion which goes on within people over different types of relationships. Inside we know when we should move away but the outer pressures are often very great and we stay instead much against our own better judgments or to satisfy the needs of society.

It is important to recognise that the taking of a life, one's own or another's is never part of the Play. The notion sometimes put around that a tit for tat existence is what karma is all about is not strictly correct. Two wrongs never make a right and there are many ways for us to discover the futility of wrong without descending to that type of retribution. It is some mens' three dimensional way of thinking but that is all.

Killing is wrong. Torture is wrong. Pedophilia is wrong. War is wrong There is never a good reason for doing it and if this were how karma worked there would be a forever downward spiral.

Just as the actors in the Play are ourselves, so the unwinding plot deals with

Karma.

Karma is not punishment for sins committed in a past life. It is the Law of Cause and Effect. For example, it doesn't matter whether you jump into a fire deliberately, are pushed by intent or fall into it by accident, the end result is that the fire will burn you. That is what fire does. It will therefore burn the 'guilty' and the 'innocent'. One therefore, has of necessity to learn about fire. We have to respect it, learn how to use it for the purpose it was created and learn how to avoid its destructive properties. If we use every tool or energy in the right way, we will be working with the Power and with the Powers of the Universe.

Karma deals with the concept of 'As you sow, so shall you reap'. So, if we tell a deliberate lie of malice against someone, that which we set in motion will eventually arrive back at our doorstep. As the saying goes, 'What goes around comes around.' We have to make atonement or reparation to everyone we have ever hurt, wittingly or unwittingly and this is all part of our Karma.

We make new karma every day as we do either positive or negative things to our neighbours and ourselves. It is important to remember that the intention is all. So if we do something with the best of intentions, whatever the result of our words or actions, the intention determines the type of karma we create.

The notion that sick people, disabled physically and or mentally are working through bad karma is particularly unhelpful. It is possible that in order to try to achieve a particular virtue e.g. humility, one decides to spend time in a wheelchair and become a third class citizen in the eyes of today's society but if so, that is a particular decision made before birth. If anything, it would denote the advancement of a person who could take on such a limiting existence. The same applies to any serious disability. And it must always be remembered that karma is not a punishment. It is the natural result of everything we set in motion.

Being ill or disabled is an experience we can all learn from and when the experience has achieved its goal, a full recovery is often possible. We just need to know that we can let it go. All too often illness is accepted and settled for even to the point of calling it 'the will of God' which couldn't be further from the truth. This attitude can serve to promote a life foreshortened whereby the individual plays the part of the invalid for the rest of their life, instead of putting the lessons learned from it into practice, and going on to a full recovery.

Accidents can happen here and they can happen *there*. What is in our heart is the determining factor. To see an individual having a bad time here is not necessarily someone up there paying them back. Everything we do, we do ourselves for our own good. No one else is involved. No irate God or divinity. It is left up to us along with loved ones and mentors to decide on which method will be the best if we are to fulfill our potential, achieve karmic equilibrium and play our part for the benefit of others within the Play. We mustn't forget we are all in the same boat. At our level, no one is perfect. We have probably all done 'bad' things at some stage in our evolution and we have now matured and grown to a stage where we can see clearly the damage we do most to ourselves in the long run if we do damage to another in the interim. It is therefore in our own best interests to be constructive rather than destructive but we are only three-dimensional beings and we have a long way to go.

Those who believe they are in their last incarnation are usually in for a shock when the time comes. It doesn't work as our three dimensional brains try to work it out. One member of a group soul may have made a great deal of advancement and need never return to the earthly experience; but they often choose to reincarnate, teach and support until everyone in their group soul has reached the same stage. So it isn't a question of knowing here and now which option will be chosen. Only time, discussion and advice hereafter will tell.

Depending how things are going, sometimes an individual will continue development on the astral or mental planes or even another planet instead of on the earth plane. It is all a learning process and some of the lessons we have to learn cannot be done on Earth. For example, it wouldn't be any good incarnating on Earth as an exercise in group awareness, where all is harmony. Another place where this is happening will teach a person how it could come about on Earth by looking into the history of that particular place and how perhaps certain individuals acting cohesively brought about great changes. We all have to learn from others as and when we can. Putting it into practice here is the real challenge we have to overcome.

The physical plane is dominated by fear, the astral by emotion and the mental by logic. The physical is also extremely limiting and is an excellent vehicle through which to experience the many challenges posed by relationships. Learning to live with each other and learning to live alone can both be very traumatic. Every life is affected by relationships. Be they intimate or distant we all affect each other for good or bad and relationships with our family members or working colleagues, neighbours or friends form the foundation on which we build - and sometimes wreck our lives.

On the astral, the emotional aspect is much deeper, stronger and has more impact bearing in mind that there isn't the same fear aspect as there is on the physical plane. Visiting the astral, we can resolve problems in relationships. We can meet, sort problems out and the very next day waken up here to having a very different approach to other people. We don't remember why the sudden turn around but it just seems so right, and so it turns out to be.

If after death we decide to have a learning experience there rather than on earth, it is much less restricting and we can learn how emotions can destroy us if they are allowed to get out of hand. We can learn that love is an energy we can use for the good of all not just a chosen few. We can learn that jealousy is a great destroyer and totally unnecessary. We can learn by example how to be creative and constructive by actually experimenting with different ideas so that when we do incarnate again we take those lessons with us. We can work with projects similar to live videos to experiment with the different ways we can work something out and see the outcome of each one, as an objective observer. By doing this we can see the whole and how everyone in the Play is affected not just the rather introverted views of ourselves and others we sometimes carry on this plane.

On the mental plane we can study and learn about practical matters. Physics, engineering, science and technology all show us different aspects of all beings and environments and we can work at a particular project which when the time is appropriate we can incarnate and bring to earth. Great inventors do this. Great mathematicians don't start their interest in their present life; they have all brought it through with the 'project' as their destiny. Lessons too are learned here about relationships. Seeing the same scenario without all the emotional entanglements helps to get things straight in our mind and teaches us the destruction caused by wallowing in negative emotions. It is easy to forget that the emotion of Love can be very negative when used in the wrong way as in possessiveness or obsessiveness often promoting that other side of love- hate, in response. We can see what is actually going on within a relationship on earth as an observer and try to understand the sometimes intertwined karmic relationships, which are being worked out sometimes at the same time.

In between incarnations we can rest and learn and travel and be beautifully creative but we still have to put matters to the test in our next experience on earth. We see people all around us who are ignorant or naturally charming, totally insensitive or full of compassion, oozing with abilities, 'knowers' and thinkers or mean spirited, narrow and ugly. It's all there if we look for it. Those who are more advanced are not always top of the class academically but as it has been said before by one who truly knows 'It is by their deeds you will know them.' The greatness of spirit is shown in the knowing eyes, the helping hand, the non-judgmental approach, the compassionate support, the inner strength, and the constant friend. Enlightened ones also have the capacity to comprehend the physics and the maths alongside their other attributes and use all their knowledge for the advancement of others. Working through Karma gives us the wherewithal to reach our objectives, along with everyone else.

Reincarnation allows us to experience and experiment for ourselves what we have learned elsewhere. There are many planets, physical planes within the universe with beings similar to ourselves in form, sometimes almost identical, often advanced, the fourth dimensional Being and those far beyond that. There are others, steps behind us. We are all children of the Creator and we have to learn to look after ourselves, grow and mature naturally without any restrictions in order to achieve holistic stability. It is that stability, which allows us to vibrate on a different level, to upgrade from three to four and upwards dimensionally.

We have to learn to control every aspect of our being in such a way that will allow constructive expansion of our range of abilities. We have to comprehend fully by and through experience, the necessity of being stable, reliable individuals who can work as a team, recognising the greater abilities of some and the earnest desire of others to reach their set levels and goals. How can we possibly work with greater, subtler energies if we haven't learned to master the few we already have? It is only when we have collectively reached this point that we can move on to greater things. Reincarnation gives us all the time and experience we need to learn that the only control we should impose is over ourselves. It gives us the knowledge of the basic excesses we all start off with and consequently the honing that is necessary to reach an acceptable level as three dimensional beings.

Due to the differences within individuals and the freedom of choice, people do not always stay within the same group soul. If one has determined to race along and has learned a great deal very quickly, they can join a group soul, which is further along the journey, taking on more responsibilities, greater challenges etc. Close bonds within the group means that those who are capable of moving on sometimes stay in order to support another until they are both at the same level when they will move on together or the whole group decides to stay together. Thus there are groups of differing sizes but whatever method is chosen the race of man on earth is not moving on until they all move on to become fourth dimensional.

There will always be Great Ones on earth for this reason, working behind the scenes; sometimes taking a pivotal role to make a difference at an appropriate time, sometimes setting the world alight but briefly, showing the way to others. But we must all work to make a difference however slight in our own individual manner.

When difficult situations hit us one after another, we often ask 'what have I done to deserve this' or 'I must have been bad in a past life.' It is probably a mixture of both. The difficulties are there to overcome and not be overcome by. There may be some karmic lesson to be learned. If it can all be thought of as positive steps for us and if we can understand that we are never given more than we can deal with, it makes the difference between biting on the bullet and wallowing in despair. If we can learn to understand that we are enacting the Play, which *we wrote*, the outcomes can be so much better, the achievements understood, the purpose fulfilled.

Our **Destiny** has to be fulfilled. For some it is taken as meaning that it has all been worked out, that we have no choice and in some way we are being cheated. Somebody up there is pulling all the strings, therefore why bother? These feelings of inevitability are simply a matter of looking at it down the wrong end of the telescope.

Destiny is simply that which we have set ourselves in order to help ourselves and the group to advance as quickly as possible. Once we can realise that the main issues in the Play have to be carried out and that pre arrangement has been done by ourselves for ourselves for all the right reasons, we can begin to have a happier life. It is quite simply that whilst we do have freedom of choice the choices were made before we came into our present incarnations. Deciding to have our own way here and now wouldn't do anybody any good and to go down that road is a totally pointless exercise.

Death and what it Means

For what appears to be the majority of people in this world, the thought of death, especially a loved one's or one's own brings an instant inner tightening, a singularly unpleasant immediate recoil creating a fear that surpasses all other fears. Death is a taboo, a subject rarely discussed, never in polite society; the ultimate in denial. It promotes a picture too frightening even to contemplate, leaving a legacy of unhealthy suppression within the subconscious.

Society sees death as a weakness, a failure in the body's design, something to be put off for as long as possible. There is nothing to compare with this, the ultimate, absolute prophecy. For many it is an abstract fear which may be based in ignorance – a fear of the unknown, a nothingness perhaps or even worse, hell and damnation if you haven't kept to the sacred teachings of man. If you keep to the teachings of all the great Masters that are truly sacred, there is nothing at all to fear for there is a life after a life, after a life, ad infinitam.

The reality is that death is quite simply a shift in consciousness. This occurs when any damage to the body is so great it can no longer sustain life or, as with the natural death of old age there is the end of an era for the returning spirit. The body, aware of the shift or the leaving of the intelligence (spirit) within is programmed to recycle itself and it promptly does just that. This is an amazing feat in itself but then the body is an amazing, intelligent machine. Programmed precisely to live and programmed precisely to die must surely make us realise that it is all part of that great eternal plan.

The spirit meanwhile understanding all about 'shifts' is immediately conscious within its remaining energy fields tied to their own particular planes of existence. There is no time span between one consciousness and another. If one is no longer here one is immediately there and with no intention of returning, there it stays and it is *there* which seems to cause all the confusion. *Where is there??*

There is different for different people. It all depends on a number of factors that contribute to determining the next step. People often wonder what goes on outside of this three-dimensional world. For the most part they are unable even to begin to imagine what life is like elsewhere and so have nothing to aim for. For some, the thought of a spirit conjures up strange imaginings of amorphous blobs floating around aimlessly in some eerie dimension, wandering around for all eternity. The notion of another type of reality outside of the physical is almost impossible to comprehend. But *there* is the reality and the Earth is but a reflection, an illusion by comparison. If one can get to grips with that concept, understanding becomes much easier.

What does it feel like?

On first passing, the individual will return to a level and a plane they remember, home and the group soul. The transition from life to death is very different from what it appears to be, viewed from the physical perspective.

Whilst death occurs in different ways, for most it is a very exciting time when it actually happens and bears no relation to the often traumatic and distressing scenes around the body. It must be remembered that whilst the body is closing down, the intelligence within may be fully alert to everything around it, seeing and hearing as if fully conscious. There follows a sudden awareness on the part of the person that something very different is happening. After a few seconds of mild apprehension, excitement mounts as the return takes place. There may be a sensation of spinning somewhere in the region of the head which then becomes so fast that the head area becomes an oasis of stillness rather like being in the eye of a storm. For a few moments there is an awareness of physical surroundings still, before a willingness on the part of the individual to go.

The spirit recognising what is happening feels elated and focuses totally on leaving this dimension, knowing the thrill of what lies ahead. With all the desire and intention it has for returning home, the flight is swift and the soul supremely happy.

For another there will be a period of coma for the physical body. The spirit, after a few moments of darkness, awakes in the new dimension.

An accident may precipitate the spirit into the astral dimension first where it can see everything that is happening around the scene and it may stay in that dimension for some little time before the intention to leave this plane takes over. Quite often the spirit or intelligence within, picks up telepathically that an accident is about to happen and leaves before the accident occurs, despite moans and groans from the body which would suggest otherwise.

When death occurs very quickly there can be shock and trauma for the spirit as well as for those left behind but as spirit can always adapt supremely to each of the energy fields it finds itself in, the distress does not last. The actual moment of death bodywise may be pronounced at such and such a time by a physician, but that isn't always the case as the spirit may have left hours before even though some bodily functions are still apparent. So whilst they may appear to be *here* they are in fact already *there*.

Marjorie Sutton

Where Do We Go?

The spiritually awakened, alert person will return to that from which they came, happy to be another step further on in their spiritual progress, knowing on their release, exactly what is happening. One of the first things one experiences on leaving this physical plane and arriving on another is the lightness surrounding everything and everyone.

The love flows, for when all are truly equal there is no place for jealousy or anger or bitterness. There is a real sense of being safely back in the bosom of one's family and there is a *natural*, normal feel to it. There will be a time to evaluate and a time to rest, a time to meet with spiritual mentors and loved ones. Those loved ones who returned before they did and loved ones who did not reincarnate this time around. There is much disbelief as they meet their nearest and dearest, wondering how they could possibly have forgotten of their existence, so close are the ties that bind them. This is always a cause for hilarity amongst the Home Players. There is always a great deal of banter on these occasions before it is time to get down to the nitty gritty, that of viewing the Home Video where all will definitely be revealed. But there is always constructive criticism and time to consider, to review, reflect and to generally take stock. If all has gone to plan they will look at how best to continue their progress and in some cases, to perhaps advance now on to a higher plane. There is a great deal of excitement and joy for some at their achievements and plans for the future but that is for the future as they will have all the time they need to put these plans into being. They will continue to take an interest in the affairs of those they left behind if love was true because the love vibration can never be broken.

The younger soul will also return to that from which they came but in this event they will possibly and highly probably stay on that plane for some considerable time to come. The younger soul will have to look at what has been learned as an aid to spiritual development. It may not be a great deal and there will be time for discussion and clarity of understanding provided by the spiritual mentors serving his group soul. He will naturally be in a suitable place for his advancement in the future, surrounded by those who have attained a similar level and as such he will be at ease with those around him.

A younger soul does not necessarily mean a young persona, a child. It means one who is still in the spiritual primary school and has much growth and development to attain. The older or more advanced soul is often present in babies and children as well as in adults but has been growing and developing longer spiritually.

At these levels form is still important to the individual spirit and form is taken by everyone including the spiritual mentors. The spiritual mentors here are not the highest of beings but are advanced enough to teach and support the individual and the group members.

These beings have chosen to do this work which is often difficult but extremely rewarding. Of necessity they understand life as it is lived on Earth. They have a deep compassion and limitless patience and will be the first to lift one who has fallen and encourage them to continue with enthusiasm. It is a little like school on Earth only here all the teachers are good, supportive and have a wealth of experience of the physical dimension.

The younger soul stays on the plane it is happy on but cannot journey to more advanced spiritual planes. Instead, those inhabiting the higher spiritual planes visit the lower planes to encourage and work with the group soul from time to time to advance the group as a whole by ensuring an appropriate programme is being carried out for each and everyone.

For the more advanced soul returning to higher planes there is a certain similarity but for him there will come a time when there is no further need to incarnate on Earth. The more advanced the soul, the more it is able to experience a variety of different types of existence on different planes and planets to further its own education. Spending time on the emotional and mental planes accelerates comprehension and awareness of the importance of the group as opposed to the individual and the soul in this situation is probably now a pupil of a Master with direct connection to the Master on whichever plane he is working.

It is here that he is taught the true meaning of love and how true love knows no barriers. He will have to put this into action on the Earth plane in due course but because he has advanced so much, he knows that all the effort and the very difficult challenges he will have to meet to learn this lesson or to teach others will be worth it. For him now there is no looking back. He knows that Love is the only way. He knows that Love is an energy, that Love is God, that he is an expression of that Love, that he is an expression of the Creator, quickening from dimension to dimension, becoming aware of the Creator within, becoming one with the Creator within. Understanding we are all expressions of the Creator and that we must all accept and respect *every* expression no matter what life form it takes, on Earth or elsewhere, is our biggest lesson and often our biggest downfall.

It is not easy for man at his present level to give love to all, especially to those who he doesn't like or agree with, regarding morals or attitudes. There is always judgement at the present level of life on earth and a sense of injustice prevails with many grievances and many divisions between not only colour and creed but also more far reaching aspects.

Ideals vary tremendously within the smallest of communities as well as within the larger global communities, leaving very little room for manoeuvre. For many, hatred is a motivating force for life and the legacy of the father lives on in the child. It is only by understanding that man is at many different points in his spiritual evolution, that he can evolve spiritually.

That doesn't mean that evil should be condoned or wrongs done to others be overlooked. We must never encourage evil or make excuses for it. It must be deterred wherever it seeks to express itself. It does mean an overall acceptance that where there is darkness, light should be shed and that when forgiveness is truly sought by even the worst perpetrator it should be given readily.

In the greater scheme of things, no one is going anywhere on their own. Advancement to a particular level by the group determines the collective souls' progression onto a higher spiritual plane. Those who have made more progress than others within the group often decide to wait whilst others catch up and in the waiting work hard to bring about that understanding we all need through that deepest of all love, true compassion, so that all may move on together.

Learning to Adjust

When a loved one leaves this plane it is hard for those left behind to continue, especially if there was a deep bond not only here but spiritually, a soulmate or a twin soul, because then there is a real feeling of being alone. Here, we see only our great loss and whilst we may try to be philosophical about the loved one being in a better place, we are not always convinced, hurt, anger and bitterness often enveloping us like a cold wet blanket. There is no simple or easy way to reconcile ourselves to that loss whilst we are still learning and even advanced souls will feel bereft for a period of time. Too often the younger soul here, may seek revenge through lack of understanding. Unable to look further than the immediate they are completely wrapped up in their loss. Herein lies the biggest dangers for mankind as hatred, bitterness and anger fuels the fires of personal anguish until it becomes a roaring torrent of destruction destroying all decent feelings.

There is always an unhappy wonder, a sense of injustice, outrage even at someone leaving whilst still young in earthly measure. Nothing is more difficult to cope with than the loss of a little one especially if that little one met a violent death. There is nothing more abhorrent than for a young life to be taken in this way. It is bad enough when the death is a 'natural' one, leaving grief stricken parents behind but for any individual to harm a child means untold personal grief for the devastated parents. This form of death is inexcusable and the perpetrators should be treated as manifesting evil and as such restrained for the rest of their lives.

It is important to recognise however that a baby or child may be small in form but that the spirit within may be great and on its release, it is no longer small, or vulnerable or alone. Some of the greatest spirits come for such a short time and can make enormous changes by their passing; changes desperately needed in this unstable world before matters get completely out of hand. Often a parent will find the courage after a tragic loss, to set matters in motion which will change the law or a nation's attitude and it is only in retrospect we see the purpose of those lives.

No matter how advanced spiritually or not as the case may be, there is always someone to meet with them, for the time of their arrival there is known. They do not spend a moment alone. When the spirit understands the danger it will leave the body, often before the incident causing death occurs.

An accident too is a terrible shock to us still dwelling in this dimension but it is not so in other realms. Remember, for everyone there is always One who knows every move you make, every breath you take, through all eternity. Be assured there is always your special Someone there to help, to guide and to walk with you on every path you tread come what may. When we are grieving sorely we often cannot cope with others around us, can only see a dark pit yawning all around us. But that Someone will never let you go no matter how difficult you make it for them. Someone who will insist on helping you to your feet when you decide to organise a sit-in. Someone who simply won't go away. Someone who loves you more than you will ever know.

Banish All Fear

So many people brought up with a tradition of places to go at death such as heaven and hell, limbo and purgatory, suffer a very real distress beyond measure when a loved one passes. The thought of that loved one suffering in one of these places as punishment or sent into the wilderness as babes simply because there was no religious ceremony before they died is agonising. It is the most terrible thing to inflict on another and religions have a lot to answer for.

We all go to that place we have earned and we will be with like minded people all at the same level. Heaven is different things to different people so heaven is not a place, it is a state of being. How could it be otherwise. Just to be happy is heaven. To be without pain is heaven. To be surrounded by animals may be heaven and so it goes on. To understand that the future is yours, that there is no death, that He is in His heaven and all is, in the Greater Scheme of Things, all right with the Worlds, is truly Heaven. Everyone is catered for. For those who could have done better which is probably all of us, there is a time to think, to learn from past mistakes, to make amends but no one is left alone and help is always available.

Not everything is beautiful however. For those considered to be evil there is also a place, for like attracts like. The youngest, most ignorant of souls may dwell on a plane of ignorance, caught up in the excesses of the human body at a very basic level. Similar to life on earth, more knowledgeable individuals seeking power and control hold sway in these realms as they do here. There is a need by those who see the way ahead difficult, to rule their own tiny dominions and the young slaves, easily impressed, are caught up in the cycle of instant gratification with a promise of the power that will be theirs. It is an individualist ideal promoting a destructive downward spiral and the atmosphere here is dark and ugly.

Marjorie Sutton

Evil exists and perhaps it was once in all of us and more advanced beings go there from their higher realms to shed their light. Change must always come from within so there is no preaching as we know it on Earth but just to see a Being of Light starts the process and when more is requested, more is given. Much work is done here by advanced beings for evil cannot be left to itself.

People still find it hard to understand how, when the body has died, the personality can look the same on another plane and are just as solid and real elsewhere as they were here. This is where religion again has a lot to answer for. Religion was created by man and whilst quoting the Masters words from time to time, rearranged them to suit their own limited understanding. Most religions not only do not explore the souls spirituality but virtually forbid the individual to do so, stressing the message, 'If God wanted us to know He would have told us.' Or 'There are some things better not to know – it is beyond our understanding – if we understood that we would be God.'

In reality it is vitally important to know what we are supposed to be doing in this world and why otherwise the seemingly pointless existence where there is no personal responsibility would continue in an endless mindless spiral with no end in sight. So we have to rely on imaginings and a purely three dimensional point of view giving us gothic horror upon horror. The mindless acts of violence and hatred done in the name of religion through the ages speaks for itself.

How do they look?

Very little in appearance changes for the recently departed spirit. We are just as much spirit here as we are there. If one were to see a loved one where they are or if they came back fleetingly, by materialising seemingly in this dimension, they would be instantly recognised. If someone died as an old person, a grandmother for example, she would appear to the child as she was when alive in order for the child to recognise her. In reality she would be a younger being, perhaps a little taller, a better figure, slightly different teeth etc, depending on how she sees herself as she is there. The power of the mind is wonderful and a lot of fun. Vanity doesn't always die with the physical body!

What happens when a materialisation occurs here is that a person living in the physical dimension 'sees' with their astral vision, not their physical sight. It appears to be the same but a detailed analysis would show a two dimensional aspect almost rather than a three dimensional one and of course the visitor would just appear as if by magic without opening a door for example. Any communication would be through telepathy so although one could hear them it isn't through the physical ears but it would seem to be the same. If however, the person still alive here does not have that psychic ability, it would appear that these 'visions' do not speak.

Paradoxically, many of those grieving the most would not wish to see their loved one in this way, some irrational fear perhaps of something they do not understand. Knowing this, loved ones who have left, keep their distance. Plus, it is difficult to get close to someone when grief creates a dense fog within the person's auric fields. Unwittingly they cut themselves off not just from people here but from their loved one there, too.

Those who have returned can pick up on thoughts from this world and know when help is needed when love and support is needed and they try so hard to help but so often the barrier of grief is so absolute no one can get through, here or there.

After leaving the physical plane there is of course a similar sense of loss for the returning soul, more of a separation though than something to grieve over. Tears may be shed but the knowledge that those left behind on earth will soon be joining them, minimises the experience and gives them something to look forward to. Sometimes the return has had to be because in their true dimension, they have ongoing work to do and so this quickly takes over their thoughts and they may quickly get down to business as part of yet another team.

There is a recognition for them too that the experience of Earth is transitory and whilst they dislike the stresses being undergone by loved ones still there, there is also the knowledge that 'it's all part of the Plan.'

For the more highly evolved, more advanced spirit it is a question too of a 'back to the drawing board' attitude if all did not go to plan. Even the greatest can go astray.

There is a bigger awareness too of the Love that passeth all understanding and a greater understanding of the greater scheme of things and the part we all must play. There is so much love sent to those that are left behind on earth because everyone knows the terrible hardships and experiences being taken on by loved ones as they seek to attain evermore spiritual growth.

Time

There is no time as we know time but there is a sense of time in a very different way. Time of course passes but it is judged more in terms of interest than of minutes and hours. People know that they have all the time they need to do whatever it is they wish to accomplish. Much is carried on in between incarnations and readily taken up again on their return from Earth.

People struggle to find a purpose in this life, questioning the seemingly pointlessness of many experiences. The physical experience is hard, very hard with very little in the way of help. The physical body itself is so limited and limiting compared to other dimensions. To begin to make sense of it all we have to take on board other concepts. Pre-life Agreements, Group Souls, Karma and Reincarnation.

Nothing is easy or simple on earth but how can we even begin to teach others elsewhere if we have not understood and learned through experience, ourselves. This is only the third dimension and there are many more to go, in other worlds and on other planets. It is imperative we all learn and grow as quickly as we can if only to avoid having to come here again. Learning to manage pain and hurt, learning only to love – everyone and everything –refining our subtler energy fields until we are ready and able to vibrate at and on another level, takes many lifetimes. And always, loved ones elsewhere are willing you to make it.

Never be afraid to ask for help. We often forget our role here and get bogged down in inconsequential matters, deviating from the planned route, adding to our own burdens. When this happens, someone will come to show you the way, if you ask. If you are willing to recognise the helper and change direction the experience will be worth it.

Death is usually seen as the ultimate parting, the worst of it being that we cannot see or touch a loved one who has returned, their experience here over. Most of the other partings we experience on Earth are in many ways voluntary but most deaths are out of our control, final, absolute. The great pity is that if we could understand life and death in different terms and see beyond the obvious we would not be so broken hearted when one of us goes back home. If we could discuss death in a meaningful way throughout our lives, there would still be upset and a bereavement to grieve through but those who leave and those who stay behind would both be much happier much more quickly, to the relief of everyone.

Whilst the subject is classed as taboo it creates unbelievable stress throughout life. This doesn't just apply to when we are dying but it can hold people's lives in an iron grip, denying people their destinies as they are too afraid to enjoy a challenge, a new venture, the thrill of exciting adventures, preferring instead caution, boredom and a life less lived.

Looked at from the right perspective we should be happy for the person going home, recognising the part they have played, the support they have given and the joy they have brought into our lives during this very difficult but temporary experience on Earth.

Death is but a shift in consciousness, a welcome break from the heavy slog of life on earth, a transitory thing, a new beginning with old friends, *the very next big adventure*.

Animals, Plants, Birds, Fishes and Insects.

So many people feel the loss of a pet as much as they might another human being and are very concerned about what comes next for them, if anything. It is important to recognise that all living things have a level of intelligence within which can be evolved just as the human being can. *EVERY* expression of the Creator's Will lives on in an ever evolving expression of itself until it reaches its full potential. Spirit is within every living thing, it couldn't live otherwise and the spiritual side of every living thing has to fulfil it's potential and it's destiny.

Marjorie Sutton

There is so much for us all to learn and to achieve in order to move on to greater things as written in the Will of the Creator. There is purpose behind every being which goes far beyond our present perceptions and far beyond this galaxy. The intelligence within a plant or an animal is not a lesser intelligence merely because it does not have our form. Form itself is still experiential but the essential essence is the important factor. A plant may be able to feel and express love much more eloquently than a human being at another level, the level to which it aspires. The human being may have to learn a great deal before it can reach those same aspirations. Even here on this plane we can learn to attune to a flower or an animal, look at its form, feel it's essence and wonder… How Great Thou Art…

Your beloved pet lives on and because here too the bond is good, you will meet again. There is much for you to wonder at when you return home, things many have never even dreamed of in a world in which most can only begin to scratch the surface.

Try looking at every form you see and really try to see a little further, feel a little deeper and let your imagination open up for you the possibilities of what happens next for these amazing creatures we share our planet with. Can you really believe they are here only for our own titillation? How arrogant if we feel that only we are important in that Great Eternal Plan. Your pet will be there to greet you when the time comes but be prepared for a revelation!

Working with the New Arrivals

A great deal of my time has been spent working with the new arrivals, in the capacity of facilitator and or counsellor to those who have recently left the physical world. For these people, death has no meaning for they are just as solid and as real as you or I believe ourselves to be. I do not work alone here. There are teams of people always available, always working hard sometimes at meeting places, sometimes in the equivalent of hospitals or places of rest.

Although the work is long and can be tiring in its own way, it is necessary for those recently removed from the earthly environment. Not everyone needs help or guidance but the ones who do may need a great deal at first. Oddly enough it doesn't depend purely on the manner of passing so much as the spiritual awareness off the individual, their expectations and their ability to adapt.

Marjorie Sutton

When we are born, no matter how advanced spiritually we may be we still have to learn to use the physical body which takes a few years. When we return we are as we were when we were on the earth plane, ten or thirty or eighty years of age for all intents and purposes and now we have to learn, in a way, to be our spiritual selves again and this can take time for some.

They are still in a state of shock or emotionally drained or apparently physically depleted in some cases when they arrive, especially those who have been severely ill before passing. Naturally it takes a number of teams to work constantly in these areas.

For many it is like coming round from an operation. They are a little dazed, bewildered, disbelieving sometimes so that there are many different ways in which they may require help.

No one is left on their own unless they choose to be. For some there is a need to simply think things through before going any further. Their manner of passing may have given them food for thought or regret if it was at their own hand. Outpourings of love will encompass every being at what is still an eventful and sometimes traumatic experience.

New arrivals have a sense of loss too. Mothers want to know that the children left behind, understand that she is all right and that she will always be there for them. Partners want most of all to let their partner know that it is OK for them to get on with life and not think they have to live it alone. Earth is a lonely enough place at the best of times. They want only their happiness because they know that they themselves are OK and want the same for those they left behind.

Children are perfectly happy and protected and if a young spirit, they will have the opportunity to progress either by returning to Earth or, depending on their programme they will discuss the situation with their spiritual mentors. More developed souls will return to being a developed soul who can also return or progress on another plane depending on their programme. So there is a great deal of activity and a great need for a deep understanding at this time.

There are those who on passing do not believe that they are no longer in the physical world. At first the resemblance is so great, they close their minds to the possibility that this is the dreaded death man is so afraid of and so they withdraw into themselves thinking that they are simply hallucinating or some such. People can stay in this state for years (Earth's time) reminding one quite clearly of the shutters people put up on any subject which they don't understand or someone, some authority, has stated that they shouldn't.

Religion has taught its followers to ignore the God given intelligence we all possess to explore our spirituality in order to keep control over the masses. People may be locked in a darkness of fear, creating myths and superstitions based on man's own limited perceptions. Clearly there are others who though surprised are extremely amazed that life simply continues and that leaving the physical body is similar to leaving a coat behind. The intelligence continues in another environment. A good analogy is that of the deep-sea diver returning to the surface, climbing back onto dry land and removing his wet suit. It is that simple.

For many there is an expectation of being judged by some personal God created by their religion. Generally, people are amazing in their religious belief systems. Some are very certain that they will meet with their God in some building rather like the Albert Hall, which will be filled with people clapping as they enter. They will then be directed down the aisle to where God is sitting and be greeted by Him as one of the Great and the Good and placed on His right hand side.

Others may believe in a universal consciousness with no personalities to greet them just a sense of peace and wonder which will surround them – automatically, the same for everybody – or is it everybody? Even these people expect 'bad' people to go somewhere else but they have conjured up a place of beautiful nothingness for themselves. Others are hoping that someone they love will be there to greet them and take them home.

There are many variations on a theme when it comes to 'the reckoning'. Not surprisingly there are those who are not too happy to discover the level they have achieved or to discover that there is no hell or purgatory – for the others of course who didn't follow the same religion!

For some, the thought of meeting a past partner or a person who has harmed them can promote real apprehension. They also now realise that there may be those who will have a bone to pick with them, now that they know the truth – what really happened – so to speak. They dread meeting a partner they may have promised something to and never kept the promise – like getting married again or not being as honest about the will as they should have been. So many worries for them now that they may come face to face with their past.

I don't think anyone needs to be too concerned over such trivialities. As Shakespeare quoted

> *'Life is but a stage and all the*
> *men and women merely actors.'*

And so it is to a great extent. People understand the part that had to be played and outside of this Earthly world, marriage and relationships are not a major consideration in the sense that we all meet the rest of the group soul and things quickly fall into place. Of course a great love never diminishes whichever world we inhabit at a given time and our true relationships will last forever. Those in this situation will meet up again quickly and with great joy.

If the love on earth was not real there is a chance of people being on different planes. They will only meet if they choose to. In the lower planes, the more likely it is that people will meet and carry on their recriminations here as they did on earth because they will be on the same plane.

Marjorie Sutton

The power of the mind is particularly powerful outside of the earth plane and that which we concentrate on we will experience. The person who wants to spend time giving adoration and worship to a personal God is free to do so. The person, who believes in a space that they can call their own, will find one for as long as they want it. Everyone will find themselves in a dimension they have earned, with people if not of exactly the same mind, certainly of the same spiritual development.

Just as we can develop in different ways here so we can there, so people are not clones or boring and we all continue to learn from others. One will continue to progress there depending on what they are trying to achieve. Some will spend their time helping others in other dimensions. Some will learn as much as they can about science, technology, maths, medicine, physics, spirituality in order to bring it to a waiting world be it Earth or elsewhere.

We are only just beginning our quest as a race and we have not learned our basic lessons too quickly or too well. Much is still needed before mankind can enter the fourth dimension, can vibrate at a higher level, can move on from the darker side and out into the light. Luckily we are never alone, individually or collectively. People existing in other worlds seek only to draw back the veil that we may understand that there is so much more and the sooner we can all understand it, the sooner we will all move on to better things.

My work is dictated by the manner of the passing. People pass over in diverse ways. Whilst their arrival in the Earth plane is mostly the same, the return often brings someone with a great deal of emotional baggage. Their means of passing vary from sudden but natural such as dying in one's sleep to the shock of an accident where the impact sends the intelligence within immediately out of body.

In between these two examples are a wide variety of experiences which means that each and everyone has to be dealt with as befits their situation. If it helps to group these different methods and experiences we will begin with those who die quietly without fuss at a grand old age.

Sleep has often been described as a short dose of death. We lose consciousness, forgetting completely about Earth for a short period until we come to when the alarm clock or some noise recalls us to this world. For those who do not return but go on to greater things, the passing is usually straightforward.

My work may be with an individual or a group who have passed in this way. When they awake to their new world it will look very similar to the one they left behind. Sometimes it takes a long time for someone to accept that death has occurred similar to when breaking bad news on earth. There is shock, disbelief, panic, denial and an overwhelming sense of 'I must be dreaming'.

When I am out of body I am aware of the time I have to work with someone but these things cannot be rushed and sometimes I have to go back again and again, night after night. There are many doing this work but just as it is here, there are some who seek the same counsellor they met on arrival just to keep the continuity going. For others there are people waiting who will take them home with them because they accept straight away the situation and are quite happy.

Of course for the sceptic there are many questions to be asked now relating to religion as well as spirituality. There may be regret for having to catch up now on things which might have been done on earth had they only know there was a life thereafter and these sessions are often full of silences as they painstakingly explore just what it all might now mean. My role is to help them explore and accept and understand that everyone is catered for.

The biggest difficulty for people is to see themselves exactly as they were on earth. They look the same, they feel the same but it is not the same. And that other world has gone. There are immediate thoughts of communication with their loved ones. How can we get in touch? Especially if those they left behind are sceptics or do not believe in communication. It is terribly hard for them when they know it is possible to communicate but that their loved ones do not wish to. Naturally, they understand but it can be so frustrating.

For those who pass after a long struggle with illness there is often a withdrawal by the spirit a few hours or even days before the body finally stops breathing. It may be that the spirit goes out and returns from time to time before the last and final exit. This can occur when family and loved ones are keeping a vigil and, desperately afraid of losing this loved one, like magnets, they draw the depleted energy fields to themselves and they keep them here.

At this stage, the outgoing spirit knows it is time to go and that everything is all right but the love for those they will leave behind compels them to return albeit briefly. They leave when people fall asleep or go for a coffee. They know they have to leave within a set time limit and so they go whilst the room is for all intentions empty. Ideally it would be more helpful to them if we give permission for them to leave. If we tell them we understand it's time to go because even the dying feel guilty about leaving loved ones on their own in a very difficult world. One can speak telepathically as well as verbally if a loved one is in a coma or unconscious, bidding them farewell with all the love in the world.

After a difficult time in hospital with pain and fear surrounding them they often awaken after the briefest of blackouts, what might be classed a few seconds only, in a place very similar to hospitals here. But there, there are no doors only archways leading into gardens where a mentor awaits. The wards are smaller perhaps holding only six or eight. The beds do not have legs. But otherwise they are very similar. There is a minimum of equipment in these wards – just the person and what they have chosen to lie upon. There is no medical equipment, no hospital smell, just peace and tranquillity and a feeling that all is well. Although the form they inhabit looks and feels the same, there are no problems as with the physical body and people who arrive here usually just want and need a good rest.

Emotionally and mentally they may be exhausted and to be free from pain and anguish, desperation and fear is simply wonderful. When they are ready they can leave and take a stroll in the gardens. There are no formal lessons or counselling sessions but when a person needs to talk there is always someone there, waiting in the most beautiful of surroundings. After the ordeal of Earth people often need time to reflect or switch off completely and always there are those who wait close by only seeking to help, giving of their time happily.

On one occasion I had an appointment in an astral hospital. I was walking quickly down a corridor looking into these wards to find the person I had come to see, when in one ward I was amazed to see an uncle of mine who had passed on ten years before. He still looked ill and was lying down as he must have when on earth just before he died. He returned my gaze but did not appear to recognise me. I didn't have time to stay but on my return journey I looked in again perplexed. He was still there alone. All the other beds were empty although there were signs of occupation, probably the occupants were visiting others or strolling in the gardens. I sent out the thought to him that his brother, my father was somewhere around. He picked up the thought and turned to look at me. He didn't seem to understand…This wasn't heaven or hell or purgatory. Where on earth was he? He was waiting because he still hadn't come to terms with his death. Ten years is nothing there of course but I had thought he might have got dressed in that time!

Those who are killed outright in an accident often cannot believe it at first. They are still there, but in the astral dimension and why can't you see them. After all they, the personality is not transformed through death. Nothing much has altered. They can see what is going on around them and they are OK. There is a brief period of totally not understanding if it is not an advanced soul, or, especially if its belief system did not entertain a life after death. It can be very frustrating like trying to fight cotton wool. They can see you, hear you, are *that* close to you. It's a little like a nightmare scenario, like watching a television screen with the sound turned off and worst of all for the immediate time afterwards, they are on their own. Once they relax and stop fighting to be heard they become aware of others around them who they will turn to for answers. People like myself who just try to be there for those returning souls. Some like me are just visitors but others live there and have chosen to do this work, remembering perhaps how difficult it had been for them too. These people are eventually led away through the corridors and onto the astral plane.

For those killed in battle when hundreds or thousands are returning hourly there is a mass situation to be catered for and it can as busy there as it is here in these situations.

Marjorie Sutton

It is amazing how some people, especially trained soldiers are still arguing the wrongs of the decisions made, the way it should have gone and the sense of disappointment almost at the outcome, rather than emotions one might expect them to feel. But because the time from here to there is immediate, it does take time to get your head together and look at what comes next.

There is a holding place where people can meet up with each other and have their own inquiry's, 'post mortem's if you like on what went wrong. A checking in place where they are directed to and which they make for in leisurely fashion. Those who were living within the middle or far eastern countries seem to take it all in their stride; are less stressed than others who perhaps didn't believe in a life afterwards and who wonder if they are simply dreaming only to come to the conclusion that they are not. It can be rather like an enormous warehouse with the ones who came across on their own, sitting with their heads in their hands, hugging themselves, crying for those they have left behind. Some are crying for themselves, a form of self pity sometimes. Others are mingling with small groups from the same village or town. There is often a sense of weariness. They are so tired, drained in every way, unable to speak, often just crashing out. It doesn't last for long but for me there is always the reminder that it is so like earth at this point.

For those who have ended their life here prematurely, there is much help but within the greater scheme of things, to self destruct is not an answer and for many when they realise this, it is traumatic in that they might have wasted a life. Not only that but they may have left others in the Play without their supporting Actor and the ripple effect is awful. The realisation of this can be very depressing but one cannot judge another and their mentors will be there to support. Sadly they have to come to terms with what they threw away, what they might have achieved in spiritual growth. No one can take away the disappointment or alter in any way the decision made. People become very lonely and afraid on Earth, maybe desperately ill and alone, maybe mentally distressed to the point where they make that final choice so just as there are many reasons, so too are there many outcomes after death. They have to come to terms with what they created and left behind in terms of inappropriately guilt ridden relatives and friends who will probably carry that guilt to their graves. It is a dreadful legacy to leave and they will probably spend time trying to send out their thoughts of sorrow to the ones left behind together with very much love and pray that they will be forgiven. For those who had reached a level of life that had no quality to it, there is still the part they had to play that finished too soon. How difficult life on earth can be and as we are not allowed to remember the plot or our own particular roles it is not surprising that many just cannot continue.

But no one is left in some limbo of man's imaginings or deserted, flung into hell or beset by demons. A loving Creator knows all our limitations and has provided for them. Counselling here can take a great deal of time for no one can reproach us as much as we can ourselves. How to make reparation? How to comfort those left in a mess? What have they learned from the exercise? Why did no one 'up here' stop them? The list of questions is endless sometimes. For others it isn't such a soul searching event but no one is there to judge for haven't we all been there one time or another? Haven't we all made the same mistakes? How else are we to learn except the hard way.

When it comes to the babies and children, the women who have lost them are in a very unique situation. Whether the pregnancy was aborted, naturally or otherwise, or the child was stillborn or died shortly after, there can be a lifetime of mourning for the child that was within and was their child just as much as the child that was born and lived. Fifty years on and a woman may still wonder and grieve. And no wonder. The spirit making contact may be very advanced, may be a major player in the group soul and the love a woman feels for her unborn child can be immense, the child truly a part of herself which disappears, is no longer there. There may be feelings of guilt or rejection or simply bewilderment which a man can never experience no matter how much they too hurt at the loss. If they could just try to understand that there are a number of reasons for this. It may be that the physical form may have a flaw and it is thought better to abandon this and try again later. It may be that seeing further down the line as it were, someone in that particular Play is heading for problems and the necessary contact would not take place, the necessary experience denied and so they decide to withdraw.

On the other hand the children who return may incarnate again quickly and to the same parents or depending on the overall Plan, meet their challenges in other dimensions. It is important to recognise that the child does not suffer at all and their mentors and the group soul take everything into account. People here naturally worry about the child who returns sometimes with dreadful imaginings of a lost little soul, on its own, crying, perhaps someone evil taking it but that does not happen. Every consideration is given to them and they quickly adapt to the level they find themselves in. The baby born to a woman is small in form but the love can be that of a fully matured soul far more developed than she was herself. The connection between will always be that of a special love even if there is no 'baby' in that other plane. There is nothing for a mother to worry about. When they eventually meet again it will be as two souls who have known each other forever.

Those souls who are spiritually young may grow up much as they would here except that their playtime is for real. For a time they can *be* Captain Cook or members of his crew, can *be* Peter Pan or Wendy and not just watch the television or read a book leaving everything to the imagination. For them

Marjorie Sutton

it is a truly wonderful world having all the highs and the lows of childhood but they are always in safe hands. The fun is fantastic, the adventure illuminating and all the players are children taking parts as only children can. Like everything on Earth, virtual reality also started here. Many children have been so traumatised before returning, through war or abuse that they need to be allowed to be children in the true sense when they arrive. There is so much love for them and they are encouraged to play with other children in this way as a means of quickly extinguishing the memories that otherwise could scar them for a great deal of time, creating an inbuilt fear of the earth plane. The energy fields they return with are often full of emotional and mental scars which would remain to cripple if this were not so.

For me there are always new things to learn, things I have never thought about within earth's dimension but which are thrust upon me as a learning experience elsewhere. One of these learning curves came about as I was working with new arrivals at an arrival point.

It was a very large building, two storeys high and it was extremely busy. Another lady and I were responsible for the flood of humanity coming back. There was a mixture of races and genders, all with their own ways of dealing with their return. People were sitting or lying alone or in groups, some animated, others exhausted. Some were chatting idly as if they were just out having afternoon tea whilst others held their head in their hands, alone with their thoughts. There was as always a war on in one part of Earth and soldiers were returning in large crocodiles along the road. They were from the Middle East and as I looked out through a window I marvelled at how they took things in their stride. The building was already full of those who had 'checked in' and I recall wondering where they were all going to go but it would not be my problem as I was due back in the Earth's dimension.

I remember feeling very tired because as well as working hard here, my physical body was suffering from a bug I had caught whilst on holiday and as my time to go drew closer, the pull of the exhausted physical body made itself known. Then, out of the blue there appeared a woman heading in my direction, striding over the people sitting around on the floor. She looked pale and drawn and her body was swollen from the hips down. I recognised her immediately as one of my clients who had been given an overdose of a strong trial drug of chemotherapy but as far as I knew she had not as yet passed on although that was inevitable.

'What a 'thing' that was,' she complained angrily. She was referring to the complete botch up at the hospital which despite her protestations had given her what turned out to be the lethal injection very much against her wishes. And now she was here! Someone trying to get into the room caught my attention. He had entered but could not get past the people near the door. At every turn people blocked his path and eventually he had to go back. It was the lady's husband. Although he had come to the right place he was neither looking at me or at his wife, just doing his best to get into this place. I turned back to her, explaining that I had to go and she understood. She had just wanted to make her contact with me. She turned and moved away as I returned to my body.

It was 6 o'clock in the morning and my physical body was weak. I lay there pondering. I decided to wait until her husband rang me with the news, there was after all, little else that I could do. I could hardly ring him with mine. It was Wednesday. On Friday evening he rang me to tell me that his beloved wife was dead, that she had been in a coma since the early hours of Wednesday morning and although he had never left her side she had not recovered consciousness. He was completely devastated. They had married later in life and had no children and he truly loved her. He was desolate. I couldn't tell him what I knew as it might have frightened him or would it have been a consolation? I couldn't take the chance of adding to his misery or fear or whatever was going through his mind. Perhaps there would be another time, another place but not now.

I sat back and wondered. I had seen him there trying to follow his wife, knowing where she was – on another level of his consciousness- trying to make contact with her telepathically but to no avail. She hadn't been aware of him and what had surprised me was that she hadn't been surprised at her surroundings or questioning them. She seemed to know exactly where she was and why. She was just so angry that this had all come about by pure arrogance and control within the medical world. Her life had come to a sudden end without her consent. I have often wondered since how she came to terms with that and what might have been left undone. I have not seen her since as far as I know. If I have I haven't brought the memory back with me. Her husband did contact me a year or so later, he thought he had been with her in a dream but the dream was so real…could he come and see me…Perhaps now would be the right time, the right place.

People who suffer bereavement sometimes have vivid dreams whereby they are with their loved ones albeit briefly. They will come and confide in me knowing I will not consider them stupid or simply refusing to 'move on' whatever that means. What they have usually experienced is a meeting on the astral plane because they are not afraid and they are mature enough not to terminate their own life simply to see a loved one again. It gives them real hope in terms of what really happens when a life here is over. Knowing that life continues and the personality with it is what so many people need to know in order for their lives to continue here. Knowing that their loved ones are at peace in the sense that they are not stuck somewhere between worlds or alone or suffering gives people here the opportunity to continue playing their part.

To continue supporting others, keeping their part of the bargain, happy in the knowledge that whilst it isn't easy, it is important not just to themselves but to the loved one who having played their part is relying now on them to play theirs. Otherwise so much has been in vain. It may not take away the loneliness perhaps or the great sense of loss but it does mean that the purpose to our existence is being met and in the meeting we are still supporting the one who has left. They are grateful beyond measure that we don't fall at this the most difficult of obstacles.

When we can treat death as normal and going home as natural, when we can see the folly of taking life on earth too seriously, when we can see the reality and not the illusion, we will truly be able to enjoy every day, living in the eternal now as we are meant to do. To be able to laugh at ourselves in the midst of our troubles, knowing that all things pass and that somebody up there always loves us would be a better way to live. Knowing that the ones up there will receive our thoughts and would like us to receive theirs would mean that the parting is not so final. That whilst it may not be ideal to be parted it is only for such a short spell of time, a blink within eternity, our lives would be so much more fruitful. The more we can open our minds to these concepts the more we can achieve and when it comes our time to leave and become a 'new arrival' we can look forward eagerly to meeting those who await us with excitement and let the party begin.

Parallel Worlds

Like many experiences in my life they have only happened once but the impact has been so great that once is enough to last many lifetimes. The day when a simple meditation transported me to another world, a parallel world was no exception. The experience in itself was the start of a number of amazing connections which have still to reach a conclusion, a journey's end, an unravelling of my own particular mystery tour.

Minutes into my meditation I found myself looking down a street, a row of terraced houses, which seemed vaguely familiar. This I hasten to add was not part of the meditation and the usual form of mind projection where one may find oneself looking at a city in the East but very much aware of oneself sitting at home.

I had left this world and arrived in yet another form of experience not dissimilar to my arrival on this earth. There was the same 'knowing' and disappointment but this time I knew I was simply out of body and not beginning another incarnation. I knew this was not yet another dimension of the physical world, neither was I on another plane of existence but somehow I knew that here again I was on course for a brand new learning experience.

As I moved slowly along looking up at the brown-bricked frontages, the shallow steps and arched doorways I suddenly had the feeling that I had gone back in time. My immediate thought was that I was revisiting the past. The street was very similar to the one in which I had been born and in which I had spent my early years. The row of houses I was looking at could have been the same ones opposite to where I had lived. The two sides of the street had been different. One side had comprised two bedroomed houses and the side of the street I had lived in were three bedroomed and therefore instead of a two up, two down, my home had been three up three down.

There was no one to be seen in the street itself. It was strangely empty, quiet, no signs of people or dogs and cats, no traffic. My street had been on a bus route, large hanging double decker buses racketing down narrow cobbled setts. But this was a little eerie. It could have been a set for a film.

I had no notion why I was there and as I looked I realised that there were a number of subtle differences, it was almost the same but not quite. This wasn't the 1940's; it was earlier but then again it wasn't that it was a different time so much but that it wasn't quite the same place. Something was tugging at my brain, my memory but I couldn't get a hold on it. I was back in time yes, but despite the similarity, it was somehow older, poorer, lacking in some way from the busy area I had been brought up in. And yet, I knew it.

I shook my head as I looked around. Why was I here? Was I supposed to meet someone? Would I meet people from the past, my past but even as I considered this something told me this wasn't going to happen.

I began to wander down the street until I stopped at a door, which in my own life would have been the door of a friend at that time. I knocked and waited. The door eventually opened but not straight into the tiny living room as I had expected. Instead a man appeared dressed in a three-quarter length white coat, sweeping the narrow hallway. He reminded me of the old warders in mental hospitals. He had a mass of dark, bushy, curly hair framing a sensitive face. I recognised him immediately as someone I knew in the present time but from the way he looked back at me I realised that he had no knowledge of who I was. Michael. I spoke his name but he just continued sweeping and eventually I moved away. I was annoyed and mystified. What on earth was going on? This was not my usual experience outside of the physical and it irked me to be brought to a place, which for all intents and purposes was not responding to me. This I now fully realised was not a step back into the past. There was no life here and Michael, as I knew him in the present time, was symbolically clearing away the last remnants perhaps from an already empty, dead house.

Marjorie Sutton

For some reason this knowledge gave me a feeling of great urgency. Something stirred very faintly in my memory. I was here to find someone, make a connection. Immediately, I found myself moving swiftly through houses, all empty, through areas and thoroughfares, searching, searching but for what or for whom I did not know. Then, when I was becoming breathless almost with the constant rushing and consternation I found him.

Peter! Oh Peter! He was beautiful. How could I ever have forgotten you, left you? I knew of course that the veil does descend between the worlds as it must but this was so different. It wasn't just meeting someone again, there was a feeling of pure disbelief that I could have ever parted from him let alone forgotten him.

He was sitting on the floor next to a round dark wood polished dining table, his back against the wall. Somewhere there were two children connected with this but my thoughts were all for Peter. This man who was my everything. Tall and slim with dark hair and dark eyes, eyes now staring into space, desolate, absolutely desolate. How could I have ever left him? I would never leave him again. Emotions of fear, of pain, of unbelievable love flooded through my being as my thoughts went out to him but even as I promised never ever to leave him again I realised with a sickening jolt that he was unaware of me. Like Michael, he didn't see me.

I thought then of my present life especially my children whom I adored but amazingly they paled into insignificance beside this man. I would stay here. They could and would get along without me. They were grown up, living their own lives, as they should. I would never return even if that meant staying in some sort of limbo forever as long as I could be with Peter.

The thought began to assert itself very strongly, the words in double block letters impinged on my sight and a voice reiterated...Parralel World...Parralel world. What did that mean, what did it entail? How could I cross into it? I was only an observer at the present moment but whatever it took I would do it.

I leaned towards him, crouched down on his level held my hands out to him, my eyes never leaving his beloved face. But he was not seeing me. I was invisible to him. A voice spoke in my ear, stressing 'You are in a parallel world.' It was a man speaking, hinting in those few words that I could not be with Peter. 'I will stay here. I will give up everything to be with Peter. Everything.' I was heartbroken but the man was already bringing me back, back to my life, my present existence. I became aware of the room I was in and tried to return, return to Peter but obstinately the room persisted in drawing me back, the words ...a parallel world...a parallel...world tormenting me until the room was fully back in focus and I sat there completely shattered.

For many days afterwards, despite me knowing that I had to live my life out here, I longed to return, to be with Peter. I was very very depressed. What had happened to him, why was he in such a state himself, why so desolate, so broken? The questions went around and around in my head unceasingly day and night. I could not sleep, could not stop thinking of Peter. Somewhere deep inside was a great emptiness and a lonely ache that would not go away.

I had been given no illuminating comprehension of the roles we had played, the lives we had lived, had no way of knowing why we were apart and I questioned it constantly. Why oh why had I been shown this if there was nothing I could do.

There had to be a reason but for the life of me nothing was clicking in even now, I am still unaware of why I had been shown him, except.......

Approximately two years later I was asked to take part in an experiment. A friend of mine who was recovering from a chronic illness wished to resume her career as a therapist. To this end she wanted to practise her therapy skills on me. A session of regression. I tried to get out of it, laughingly telling her that I didn't altogether have much time for the concept of regression as practised, the collective mind being responsible for most regression if not all. People were only too happy to go back into the past and be someone else. It was too much like coincidence that most I had spoken to and read about involved with this experience, were in fact only changing one lot of problems being experienced now for the same problems which had happened in the past, only dressed in different clothes. The problems they experienced, situations they found themselves in were uncannily similar here and now but in a past life there always appeared to be more glamour.

However, she persuaded me to help her and just go with it. I promised that I would do my best. Do my best not to laugh or to start deliberately making things up but I did remind her that I was an author!

The morning arrived for my appointment. I had been very busy and only just managed to arrive in time. I sat in her therapy room where, like the true professional she was, all was ready for me. I told myself to behave and work extremely hard to do exactly as she said. She seemed a little nervous but she wired me up, set the tape recorder on and I settled down to listening and going with the flow in her comfortable leather reclining chair.

I listened as she counted me down in a slow gentle voice, telling me to go to my favourite place via a series of steps. I couldn't wait and went straight to the spot I always go to for quiet autosuggestive or guided meditations. So there was I, sitting on a rounded boulder by a gently flowing stream. As I looked to my right I could see a path fringed by trees reaching over the water. I heard my friend's voice but before she got to ten a man appeared, suddenly, imposing himself over my imagination. A man in a long cream coloured robe with dark curly hair, dark eyes. I was more aware of his face and the top of his body as he stood looking down at me gently smiling. This was no imagination or visualisation. He was beautiful and for the next few seconds we simply looked at each other and then my friend was instructing me again and he had gone.

I turned my attention to her voice and waited to see what if anything came into my head. Immediately I was in a familiar place. I wore a very simple long robe, had long blonde hair and I was walking to where children were playing near to a water well. A man walked ahead of me carrying a pitcher. He wore a sarong type garment and his head was shaven. We were a community of Essenes. I looked around me with interest, relating what I saw to my friend. Everytime she asked a question I seemed to know the answers at the same time wondering if I was making it all up. For an hour we continued in this way, much information coming from me as to the life and lifestyle of those times. She asked me about my family. I had two children but as a community we all looked after the children so as not to get too attached to them. From the age of four they became community children and later the boys would go away to live a life of meditation. Learn the sacred symbols and rituals, live amongst older monks of the order. She asked if I had a husband. I spoke about 'my man'. He had gone away and had not returned. I didn't know when he would. He had some mission to accomplish about which I knew very little. She asked me about a man called Jesus. Did I know of him? I did but not a lot. I had seen him only from a distance as he had passed along the road below where we lived and a number of people had followed him. My man had become involved with this Jesus but I knew nothing more that I could tell her about him.

More questions about life at that time, ideas, lifestyles and then, in a break towards the end of the session I found myself in a place, a room of stone, At the far end were two people with a body laid out between them on a stone slab. They appeared to be attending to this body as some requirement for burial. My friend asked me to describe certain aspects of my surroundings, which I did and then she asked 'Is it Jesus?' 'No I replied but people are meant to think that it is.'

We moved on and I found myself in a darkened hut, much older now, lying on a bed and quite calm. I was alone and I had come here to die. My man had never returned. She asked how I felt about my life. I said it was OK. There was nothing special about it and it was normal to die. I wasn't worried. I was on my own now here. It was time.

She then began to bring me back telling me that I was going to return to the present time, counting back slowly from ten to one. As we reached about six I jumped, startled, unbelievably excited. The man I had seen at the beginning of the session was here again but briefly. 'Peter' he was saying…'Peter…The Rock'. Of course. I recognised his beautiful face. My Peter from the parallel world. The first time I had seen him, for some unfathomable, unbelievable reason it hadn't registered but now, once more I wondered how on earth I didn't recognise him before.

Marjorie Sutton

Perhaps I would have been too excited to continue with the session and the veil had remained down until the session was over. So the session was important? True? Peter was certainly real.

I opened my eyes and looked at my friend eager to tell her that whatever may or may not be real about my 'regression', he was very real. I was so excited. I recounted the tale and she listened carefully. She then explained her own feelings.

Before I had arrived at her home that morning, as she prepared her therapy room making sure that everything was just right, she had become aware of an influx of energy. This had heightened her own receptivity, making her a little nervous, wondering what was going to happen. When we had begun and she was counting down, the monitor I was wired up to showed her that I was in a relaxed state. Then it charged upwards and she had feared that I would not be able to continue as I appeared to come out of this happy state into one of excitement. It had happened shortly after the session had begun, had coincided with the original arrival of the man, Peter.

I marvelled with her at this amazing development. She knew nothing of Peter or the parallel experience, no-one did and I was just so delighted. She switched off the tape and wound it back. Switching it on again, we found that nothing had been recorded! I wasn't bothered too much about the tape not recording but she had realised at some point in my description of things I was seeing that she was sure she had photographs of such a place. She would also have liked to verify what I had said at a later date.

Her photographs she had taken on a visit to the holy land. Sure enough as she found the photograph album, it was all there, the stone room especially with its stone table at one end where the dead were cleansed and robed for burial. I had never visited the Middle East or seen photographs of the area, so she was quite certain that I had indeed been regressed. I wasn't bothered one way or the other, my only thought was for Peter and he was for real.

I went home and sat in a chair by the hearth. I had left a couple of tapes I had found in a drawer earlier on the side table. One of these I wished to listen to again but the one I picked up now to listen to was one I had never heard before. It had been given to me along with a few others from someone who thought I could re-use them instead of buying new, so there was no mystery as to how the tape arrived in my home. It was just that I hadn't actually listened to what had been previously recorded.

Someone was singing. As I listened I realised that it was Iris Williams singing 'He was beautiful' I had never heard it before but it seemed to convey all the right words, conjure up all the right images surrounding Peter. I couldn't believe it. I played it over and over again until I knew the words by heart. Not Coincidence or Chance but Synchronicity.

Two years later I found myself on a holiday of a lifetime. The offer had come completely out of the blue and I found myself on the island of Penang, Malaysia. One morning, wishing to capture a beautiful sunrise on camera, I sat by the sea wall as the sun rose. I got my picture and sat there watching the unfolding life about me.

As the sun rose over the water so too did the people around me begin to take shape. The Chinese people were out taking their early morning exercise. Tai Chi was in progress and a solitary Hindu made his salutations to the sun. As I watched this beautiful peaceful scene, I became aware of four Buddhist monks about to pass by where I was sitting under a tree. Three of them looked to be in their early twenties, their saffron robes beneath their shaven heads, dipping down to thonged feet completing this idyllic picture. The fourth who passed nearest to me wore his robe wound cowl like around his head, his profile old, stern, their Master perhaps. They came to a halt a few feet away from me, the old monk sitting almost facing me under another tree whilst his pupils rested against the sea wall. They were chatting quietly and after a little while I looked across at them again. The monk sitting, still with the robe around his head, had changed completely. He was beautiful and young. He was smiling at his friends, at something one of them had said. I couldn't get over just how beautiful he was. The cowl had been lowered and he had light brown, wavy hair under the cowl and he didn't look Malay or Chinese, looking far more western than his friends. But his beauty just took my breath away and I had to turn my face away in case he saw me staring so.

Secret Journeys of the Soul

A few minutes later and they were returning back the way they had come. Again they passed where I was sitting, chatting happily. The hooded monk passed close by me once more and I looked up at his profile. Stern again, much older than the others. I couldn't believe it. The change was phenomenal. He wasn't taking part in their banter and as they passed me I raised my camera to take a photograph. I hadn't dared to take one in full view of them as I didn't want to offend them, so I made do with a photograph of their receding backs. It would still be a nice picture for my album.

For some reason I moved across a few minutes later and sat where he, the beautiful one had sat. Immediately there was a sense of peace embracing me. Is that how he feels, all the time, I asked myself, in wonder. And then the view across the water altered. Mist arose between the island and the mainland and I was transported into a sensation of great upliftment. Of knowing that whilst everything was not right at this time, in the greater scheme of things everything was still on track. That sense of peace that passeth all understanding pervaded my space. I seemed to be suspended between two worlds and I knew that this young/old monk had in some way had a great deal to do with it.

All too soon it was time to return to my hotel, pack up and return to the apartment in Kuala Lumpur on the mainland. The first thing I did the next day was take in my full roll of film from Penang to be developed. A day later it was ready. I viewed the photographs with great pleasure until I came to the last one. It was the one of the retreating monks only instead of four there were only three! The one with the cowl had not appeared in the picture despite there being lots of space on the path.

He had been so beautiful. Was he Peter? Had Peter come to me again in a totally different way this time but a way that could never be forgotten? His face, the monk's had not been the face of Peter from the parallel world or the face of Peter from my regression, which had been one and the same, but the immediate words that had sprung to mind were exactly the same. He was beautiful. Never a way in which I have ever described a man before, never thought of as relating to a man as beautiful but each time the same phrase had raced through my mind.

As I looked down at the photograph I knew that whoever he was he would always be conspicuous by his absence. The threads in this particular tapestry seem to me to be drawing together but what the final picture will reveal is too exciting even to contemplate. I will simply await the next experience for there will surely be one.

Encounters in Outer Space

After working for so many years in the dimensions around earth and occasional visits to higher spiritual realms, it came as something as a surprise to find myself one night outside of my body but in yet another totally different way.

As I became aware of my surroundings, I literally felt different. I knew I wasn't in my physical body but neither was I in my astral or mental field either. I certainly wasn't experiencing a spiritual dimension, which only left? I wasn't sure although the question persisted in my head but for some time I was so amazed at what I was seeing that it didn't seem that important.

I was standing somewhere in outer space! It was nothing like anything I had ever seen or envisaged from Space documentaries on the television or views from the telescopes in strategically placed viewing sites around the world. At first my eyes feasted on the sights around me, the feelings which were invoked and the wonder at what I was being shown. At the outset I became aware of a man in black standing with his back to me, his hands resting on the top railing of a rounded balcony overlooking the platform he was standing on. He was very tall and although seeming to be Caucasian his hair was also very black, cut in style that might be seen anywhere on Earth. Very handsome. I was standing somewhere on something – a platform or similar because I was able to look over and down – but the scene that surrounded me took all my attention. He didn't seem to know that I was there, he certainly gave no intimation of it. I was standing behind him and to his left by about twenty feet or so.

The beauty of the scene was beyond words, drawing the whole of my being into that of truly feeling at one with the universe. There was also a feeling that there were beings living out there. It was in fact teeming with life even though I couldn't from this distance detect the smallest glimmer. Great globes of light I knew were planets, shone in pale colours, dotted amongst smaller, more sparkling stars. I felt that I could have reached out and touched them and yet I knew they were quite a distance away. I could never have begun to imagine the scene around me. No memories here from 'star trek' adventures. It was just incredible, like nothing man has ever seen before. There wasn't the distance one experiences when viewing the beautiful night sky from Earth where although one can see quite large stars sometimes, one knows they are light years away and even the comets that come close were nowhere near as large or as bright. Bigger than the moon and with such energy but not like energy from our sun. Looking at the moon from Earth it looks solid. Looking at the sun there is a feel of gas all around it but these were so different. Big, bright and beautiful they just took my breath away. They were so close and in some strange way I was in the middle of them, just standing there on this platform. It was pure magic. There was no sound but the atmosphere was alive. I wasn't in my astral body because I could only see what was in front of me within my line of vision, similar to when in my physical body. I had to turn to see what was on my left. As I slowly drew it all in it was like breathing in eternity. It was just the most wonderful experience. It felt physical. I knew automatically that I was not within my own galaxy but I didn't know where I was or in what direction or how far I was from anywhere else. It didn't matter. I certainly hadn't died and gone to heaven but it seemed like the next best thing.

This was not a dimension around the Earth nor was it in a higher spiritual realm. It was in the physical world and so was I – almost. Something was different but to all intents and purposes it felt physical. How could I stand on a space platform without any sort of wearing apparel we are shown on Earth? And how could he?? Everything about me seemed stable just as it does when standing on Earth, even though we know the Earth is revolving at an extraordinary rate of knots, we know we don't feel the spin or the motion. But I and the man – I looked across again – were standing quite still; a part of it all. Why had I come here?

As I turned slowly to my left and looked about me, I saw some way below me a large ship rather like an aircraft carrier seen at sea on earth. It was huge and although it too appeared close by I knew that it was still some way away. Whilst the space around me was filled with colour and light and beauty, this carrier was of a brownie grey colour, very much a utility vehicle, completely flat on top but bevelled below. It was so big I couldn't believe it could stay afloat in space. I saw along the side facing me, quite high up near the 'deck' were a series of portholes almost, which looked quite small but as I watched two or three space ships came along and darted through them into the hold rather as swallows might dive into a hedge. I knew that this was a filling station where spacecraft came to refuel. I have no idea what sort of fuel and I am not technically minded but again as I watched after a period of time they or similar ones flew out of portholes presumably on the opposite side of the carrier and off into space. At the back of the carrier, although I couldn't see, I knew there was a much larger entry for bigger vehicles, rather like those I have seen on ferries. Sure enough, larger ships approached, slowing down and almost stopping, forming a queue. They were all shapes and sizes, rather like lorries, cube shaped but without the wheels and some made up of perhaps a couple of different sized blocks. This I couldn't understand because they were not streamlined or aerodynamic. Just a plain grey colour like all the other craft that I saw. That really made me stop and think. Was I dreaming? I knew I wasn't but all I knew of aircraft was that it had to be aerodynamic and these larger craft did not have that shape. As I looked down I could see the top of the carrier, the deck, quite plainly. There was nothing built into or onto it. It just seemed the cover for the ship.

Eventually I turned to my right slowly, still feasting my eyes on the scene before me. Where on earth or not on earth, was I. As I looked over to my right I became aware again of the man. He was very tall about eight feet tall, standing on what appeared to be a balcony, his hands resting on a rail, looking out pretty much as I was at the scene around him. He was dressed all in black with black hair, looked very human although I could not see his face at all. He was wearing black trousers or it could have been an all in one suit. The collar on his jacket was in the style of mandarin and very severe. His build was perfect for his size. As I looked at him, he turned and as he did so I appeared to be right behind him. As he made for the stairs leading down in what I could now see was a deck of some kind I followed him in down the stairs and through the door. Neither of us had spoken or used telepathy. We just went through the motions because that it seemed is what we always did when we met. Perfectly normal, business to do, time to be used to advantage.

Marjorie Sutton

I knew nothing more until what seemed to be much later. I opened my eyes, back in my own bed. I could not remember anything which had happened after we went inside what I now realised had been a space station. I must have been out of body in my etheric field, hence the different feel to it. It operated very much like my physical body in the sense that it only had two organs each for eyes and ears. If there were any more they had not been used. But there were not the multifaceted receptors of the astral body. The etheric is the exact double of my physical body so that made sense. I hadn't known that I could actually take my etheric field with me as this was very much attached to the physical. This was yet another learning experience, which needed a lot of study.

In the weeks that followed I spoke at some length to a few of my more technical minded friends who said immediately that outside of the earth's pull, craft would not need to be aerodynamic and they accepted quite happily the scene I had painted for them. Plus the etheric or bio plasmic body as science now calls it probably could exist quite happily in an otherwise physical/ etheric space environment.

A couple or so years later I was sitting waiting for a friend who needed some healing when I became sharply aware of two spacemen standing in front of me both wearing spacesuits and helmets just as one might see on the telly. One looked like the all-American boy, clean cut, dark hair, handsome. I could his face clearly. The other was very different. 'What our your names?' I asked. One of them seemed to be saying

'Anatobin' and it took some time for me to pick up the name as the pronunciation didn't seem quite right but the other name came back quick as a flash 'Budgie'. His profile behind his helmet looked similar to that of a budgie and I smiled. Was this a nickname or someone of a different species.

'Why are you here?' I asked. 'To heal. We can you know'. I smiled and said OK before they disappeared.

On two or three other occasions they and two others both looking perfectly human have appeared to me in this way which of course has given rise to a great deal of wonder because these people are not dead. They are very much alive but from another galaxy and yet I was picking them up with my etheric vision presumably. And where were they? Did they live around us in the etheric fields around the earth. Were they one step on from us, able to come and go as they pleased between the etheric and the physical? Another pile of questions all begging more questions for me to address in the coming months and years.

Another couple of years passed and I was to see the tall dark man from that other galaxy again. This time I had invited a friend who was in great distress to my home for a meal. She was expecting to have her foot amputated and was in a great deal of pain with her leg which had an area of about one and a half inches which was little more than a hole with a patch of necrosed skin across and around it spanning about 2" in circumference. It was about three inches above her ankle and was the result of years of problems with her deep veins after undergoing a large operation. Shortly after we arrived at my home I became aware of another in our midst by a feeling of very strong energies around me which agitated my whole being. As my friend was a medium herself it didn't' alarm her when I informed her of this.

Five minutes later I became aware of a very tall man all in black standing in front of her, his head reaching through the ceiling although it was the ceiling which disappeared. He was about eight feet tall. I recalled the man on the space station and wondered. Then, in front of me there appeared three very blonde ladies wearing long white robes and something in their hair. Facially they looked very much alike. They were sitting on a large pouffe situated in front of the long couch my friend was sitting on. They appeared to be waiting, seemingly wanting to get on with something. Telepathically I was told to position my friend in the long couch with me at her side. She was to position her feet over my lap so that I could just make contact with the sole of the naked foot on the damaged leg. This I did and the healing began. It took about fifty minutes and I didn't see anyone in that time or even guess at what they were doing. She went very deep, breathing rhythmically whilst my hand became colder and colder. In the end I had to take it away from her foot as the cold was beginning to burn. Then I was told that she must act as if her leg was in a plaster cast moving as little as possible for four days. She always had bandages on this leg to prevent the skin from being harmed further and now I was told she must not remove the bandages for any reason until the fourth day. Twenty minutes later she came round and the energies were back to normal in my room. They had gone.

She immediately knew something special had happened and was very excited. I explained to her what she must do and the importance of following instructions which she agreed to do and I drove her back to her home. On the fourth day I drove to her house where a group of like-minded friends were meeting. We all waited as she unravelled the leg bandage but no one gasped as much as she did when she saw the result of the healing. The leg was perfect. The flesh was firm and as pink as that of a baby. No sign whatsoever of the discoloured green and brown necrosed area, no pain, and no inflammation, no grey hole. Not surprisingly she cried tears of joy. So much for all the talk of aliens out there only intent on war and personal gain.

About three years later I was sleeping over at the same friend's house. After retiring to bed I found myself out of body looking through the bedroom window. I was not in my astral body and it wasn't my physical but so nearly the same. I was in my etheric field again for only the second time. As I looked out and up at the starry night sky I became aware of two bright lights moving quickly towards the Earth, one a few 'years' behind the other. They were on their way. Telepathically I was told that these two bright lights were many spacecraft, which would reach our dimension in a few years time. As I watched I was suddenly transported again to what seemed to be the exact spot I had visited on the first occasion. I was back on the space station. The man in black was in exactly the same place as before, looking out over a kind of balcony. Was he waiting for me? I rather think so. I looked about me as I had done the first time. The filling station was there in just the same place and for some time I breathed in the glorious beauty around me before moving over to the tall man but this time I recall that as he turned I was already speaking quickly to him. About what I do not know but I do know I was there to report on something or to give him information but on what I have no idea. We walked down the steps again and entered through the door and just as before that is all I can remember until I opened my eyes once more, back in this galaxy. I didn't sleep the rest of the night, there were too many questions going unanswered but I told my friend the next morning. 'Hope you said thank you' she said, 'for my healing'. Mmm I hadn't thought of that – as far as I know.

I have witnessed many spacecraft and unidentified flying objects since a child, mainly in the north west of England but never a flying saucer. Oddly enough a client of mine where the first two spacemen had appeared to me has also had that experience. She drew it in detail and said it had shown her that there was so much out there she had never dreamt she would ever see or even believe in. It really took her breath away. Her life changed with her understanding and she became more contented, knowing that as she approached her own return (she was in her 80's) she had so much to look forward to.

I recall when Hale-Bopp comet came around. It just appeared in the sky one spring day and I watched it for days afterwards, remembering my own travels into outer space with a great longing. So much out there, so much to know, so much going on, so many questions left unanswered but I have no doubt it won't be for long.

Many people, especially UFO watchers and fanatics have asked me if I have seen the 'little grey men'. The answer is No. That doesn't mean of course that they do not exist. So much exists but I cannot help but find it sad that so many people are preoccupied with spacemen and wondering what they look like, hoping for a different life form when this world of ours is teeming with amazingly different life forms. Why do people not try to communicate with *them*. If one actually listens to an animal or a bird and attunes to it one can almost understand what is going on. Telepathically it is possible. When I lived in the country I used to spend a lot of time experimenting with the village dogs and the local birds just watching, attuning and listening and I was delighted to listen to their chat and their debates and their rivalries. They don't speak a language but thoughts are thoughts. These can be transformed by the human brain into the nearest words that each of us will understand no matter what language we speak because we are all spirit, all having a certain level of intelligence within, some creatures having more advanced abilities than man at the present time.

I have seen others who live in outer space on other planets but only a few. Enough however to marvel at not only how they look but how they make me feel. The respect, the dignity, the love is almost tangible and it would be wonderful to live amongst some of them for a time and learn. They are not human in form but so advanced. The difficulty in trying to describe other beings from other dimensions via the spoken word is often indescribable. If I said some were plants the brain would instantly imagine plants as we know them which would be far from the truth and a wrong idea would be given out. In some presences words are quite inadequate, it is as if in some small way, one becomes that being yet remains quite quite separate. Little grey men would be much more simple to describe. In the main, it seems that despite a following in UFO circles man still has no imagination when it comes to other life forms. We see in films about space and starships etc, people or robots of a mixture which look absolutely ridiculous instead of looking at life forms around us now which have simply moved on. One has to have the flexibility within spiritual perception to even begin to open our minds to what lies out there. I am just so privileged. If I hadn't been shown or perhaps reminded, then I would be blinkered in my vision too.

If we could just begin to understand ourselves a little more we would have a chance when it comes to creating other life forms in our imagination but that is probably for the future or when the little grey men everyone wants to see come along and pass their family albums around!

Staying Put

From time to time throughout my life I have been shown that no matter what happens I will not be allowed to return home until my work here is done. Never knowing what that work was, I have never had the luxury of knowing where the road and the work will lead from one year to the next. It has been fascinating however, to recover 'miraculously' from illness and accident in many diverse ways, even when I have clinically so to speak, had a foot in the door marked Departures.

One of these great escapes involved a traffic accident. Although I had been hit half a dozen times by an articulated vehicle which did not stop or brake and my car was a write off, I and the car came to a halt, thrown to the side of the road, me relatively undamaged. Despite glass and metal splintering all around me in this gothic horror roller coaster of a ride, narrowly missing other cars by inches and seeing the frightened faces of children looming around me, no one else was injured. I received no cuts or abrasions as the car continued to crumple in on itself. I did seriously hurt my skeletal system and the shock to my body was great, but I hadn't been killed or seriously injured in any life threatening way. It took me six months to return to work, to self heal and begin to walk again; to return slipped discs to their original place and to be able to move without pain. Through self healing, I eventually got over the shock and regained the use of my right arm which had been damaged resulting in paralysis. I was very grateful. I had not been concerned about dying during the accident but I had prayed that I wouldn't be hurt! Ever the wimp.

A SOCO who contacted me later to enquire after my health informed me that there must have been at least a dozen up there who had been looking after me. The nature off the impact in other similar incidents normally broke people's necks and death was the usual result of such an accident. I knew that someone had intervened and I made a silent wish…If only I knew just what it was all about. If only I could thank them personally.

One Sunday evening four months after the accident, as I arranged a tray for dinner and switched on the TV to watch a favourite programme of mine, I suddenly became aware of a presence. The atmosphere in the room had taken on a subtle change. I began to eat and watch the television but not for long. The presence was overpowering and tears began to flow down my face. Ever since my accident I could cry with little or no provocation for just a couple of minutes which I recognised as post traumatic shock and this occasion, I thought, was no different. I couldn't have been more wrong.

The presence became stronger and I knew that I had to switch off the TV. Shoving a tape in to record the programme I sat back to speak to whomever it was who had arrived so swiftly and so powerfully and so out of the blue. The atmosphere was pulsating and the colour of the room had taken on an amber like glow. I expected the person to manifest, materialise at any moment. He was sitting on the couch that was at right angles to my chair as I looked across. I stared hard until I realised who the visitor was. It was my father. I was shocked for I hadn't expected him. My tears were still flowing and although he did not materialise into the physical I could see and feel his presence. There was no doubt of it. I listened, spellbound, as he began to speak.

He it was who had saved my life on that fateful day. February 7th. He had done so to make reparation for his time with me on earth. To make up for all the times he had never been there for me, for all the mental cruelty he had inflicted upon me, for never being the father he should have been. I could feel the emotion, the love and the remorse hitting me like shock waves across the room. My tears were still flowing, burning my face as they have never done before or since. I knew that he had been making reparation for years now and I thought he had made full reparation. He had often made his presence known in very physical ways at the same time showing me how he was helping me at work, within the house;

protecting me from a distance. And over the years my feelings for him had changed from intense dislike to first an understanding, then an acceptance and then affection. With affection came forgiveness. He was a man who should never have married, never settled down. He had wanted the life of an adventurer. His army record was impeccable, he had been brave and was a first class shot with the rifle. Meeting my mother and leaving the army was the worst things he ever did I fear. A healing had certainly taken place over those years and I bore him no ill will and hadn't done for a long time. He had been the only person I had ever hated but because of his endeavours over many years I could honestly say that I loved him now. I couldn't believe that he felt that despite all his efforts he had still needed to go that step further.

He told me of how he had been given the chance to advance to a higher plane but he had chosen to stay close to the earth in order to make the difference when the time came. February 7th. 1997. He explained. He had chosen to give up his life in order to save mine just as he might have been asked to when he was pursuing his career as a soldier. 'No greater love has a man than that he give up his life for another.' The tears flowed even faster, burning into my skin as I sobbed at the impact of his words. By his life he meant giving up the opportunity to go on ahead in his world, advance onto a higher plane and leave this vale of tears well and truly behind and he had done all that for me. I knew exactly, probably more than most, just what that meant to him. He had truly made the ultimate sacrifice for me. Listening to him speaking telepathically I heard for the first time in this life another person being completely honest about their feelings and their feelings for me. Often people will say beautiful things to each other but we never know at the time whether there is a hidden motive, whether the love is that of a genuine nature or is more of the cupboard variety.

We never know what is in another's mind. But here and now, I did. The words he spoke came from his very soul, reaching across all the levels and I found it so very difficult to cope with. He spoke slowly with humility. The emotion, the honesty was more real than anything we can normally experience during our lives here and for me it what the most profound moment of my life.

He stayed for an hour and then it was time to go. I waited as the room came back to normal. The light outside had grown dim but I sat in the enclosing gloom for another hour trying to take in what had happened. Eventually I got up and went to the bathroom. My face was scarlet and very sore to touch as if the surface skin had been taken off. My tears eventually stopped but the emotion within my body held sway. My father had saved my life. Tonight he had shown so much love, real, selfless love that I could accept was all of those things and the experience had been literally out of this world. It was many more hours before I could sleep. I have never known anyone as I knew him that night. I awoke to wonder where he was now, what he was doing and had he now made full reparation in his own mind. I hoped so because I wouldn't have asked anyone there to make such a sacrifice just as I wouldn't dream of asking anyone here to make it. In fact, there it was far more important. How could anyone love me that much? It was a very humbling thought, one which evoked much emotion, an emotion it is almost too difficult to comprehend.

For weeks I pondered on this amazing meeting with my father. How fortunate I was, how deeply moved I had been and I wished that I could have seen him physically, touched him, seen the look on his face. He would have been able to see me all right and he would have been left in no doubt just how much he had touched my mind, my heart and my very soul.

The following year I returned to my home one Sunday in the late morning to do some work after a visit to a friend's house out of town. I walked through the living room, to return a few minutes later to discover that a flower had removed itself from a vase and lay alongside it. I smiled and said 'Okay, what's all this about?' Receiving no immediate answer I sat for a few minutes and waited. Nothing. As people were arriving for a meeting within the hour I had to get on with my work. I thought of the date. Was it someone's anniversary and were they just saying Hi? I went upstairs to look in an old diary but there was nothing. As I was replacing the book in the chest, a document fell out. It was my fathers death certificate. On it was his date of birth, a date I had never ever remembered or in the past wanted to remember. February 7th. I felt stunned. My accident had been on his birthday! Some coincidence! He had given up his life to save me on the anniversary of his birthday. I should have known all along who had come to my rescue! The flower had brought it to my attention on this his anniversary. He was still around gently remonstrating with me no doubt. No doubt he thought me extremely hard work! But obviously worth it.

In Conclusion

Many years have passed since I arrived to begin my earthly experience. Most of those years have been fraught with the usual setbacks, heartache and heartbreak, which seems to be the lot of mortal man. If I have been privileged to live a double life I haven't led a privileged existence here. There has been the usual pain and tears, joy and happiness going around in its eternal cycle just the same as others have to contend with. I have learned to curb my impatience with those who abuse power and wealth; learned to tolerate those who cheat and lie and hopefully through my healing work I am putting back into life rather more than I have taken from it. That at least has always come naturally to me and gives me feelings of great privilege and humility to be allowed into another's life who is suffering. To know that a mother allows you close to her beautiful but sick child is the highest of compliments anyone can be paid because it is the ultimate in trust.

Marjorie Sutton

As I look back and recall my arrival, my horror, my despair, I still wonder what life here is all about for me, yet I know that I have indeed been blessed. I have met the most courageous and beautiful people anyone could hope to meet, my clients in my role as a healer. I have been privileged to share some of my own experiences in a way that has helped those about to return. I have helped to alleviate their fears and given some of them a new lease in life, albeit the next one.

I have learned from all the people I have tried to serve in this way. Their courage and strength has moved me to tears and left me gasping with admiration. I have learned that people are amazing, capable of that committed, selfless love for others, we call compassion. A love which is found in all cultures, families and individuals who spend their lives working around the world tirelessly to help those caught up in wars and famines with no thought for their own comforts. These are the truly advanced souls, the enlightened ones who may profess no religious belief but demonstrate their innate ability to love as the Masters teach. 'It is by their deeds ye shall know them.'

I look back on my life so far and remember the stars that helped and guided me. My amazing grandmother and my grandfather, that rock of a man and my dog Queenie who they introduced into my life and who changed my life so completely we could have been twin souls. They were the greatest influences for good in my life. They taught me how to live and how to love and how to pick myself up time and time again. How to carry on a step at a time knowing for sure that whatever crashes around me, whoever chooses to leave even at the most inopportune moment, all I have to do is keep on keeping on until things are back on track again.

I will I am sure, be eternally grateful to my friends and spiritual mentors in other realms who have made sure that I not only stay here but stay on the path until my sojourn here is complete. I marvel at the wonders of the world, this and many others our awesome Creator created for us and whatever the reason for my existence may prove to be, I have led the sort of full and active life most can barely dream of.

One day all will be revealed and I have to admit to a little apprehension. Did I keep my Play on track, play my part to the very best of my ability? The more knowledge I have the more the responsibility I have to account for.

My spirit still quickens at the touch of a new born babe, another whose arrival may just make the difference and I always wonder just what they are thinking, how long they will stay. And I hope for everyone's sake that they are in the right place at the right time.

Looking Back

I wandered awhile down memory lane
And looked at the past with new eyes
I saw once again my grandmother's love
Peeping out of her pasties and pies

I thought of her family, seven in all,
Into whose lives I was thrown
And as I sat digging and picking at bones
It struck me how much time had flown

The memories uncovered I laid side by side
And marked them with flags red and blue
Denoting the Ones I thought I had known
And the Ones I now know, never knew

Faces and places, joy, laughter, pain
Following me on through the years
Brought back to my memory the thrills and the spills
The Loves with their hopes and their fears

I looked at my life and I looked at my past
And wondered what others would see
In a personal archealogical dig—
Would anyone find the real me?

ISBN 1-41204517-7